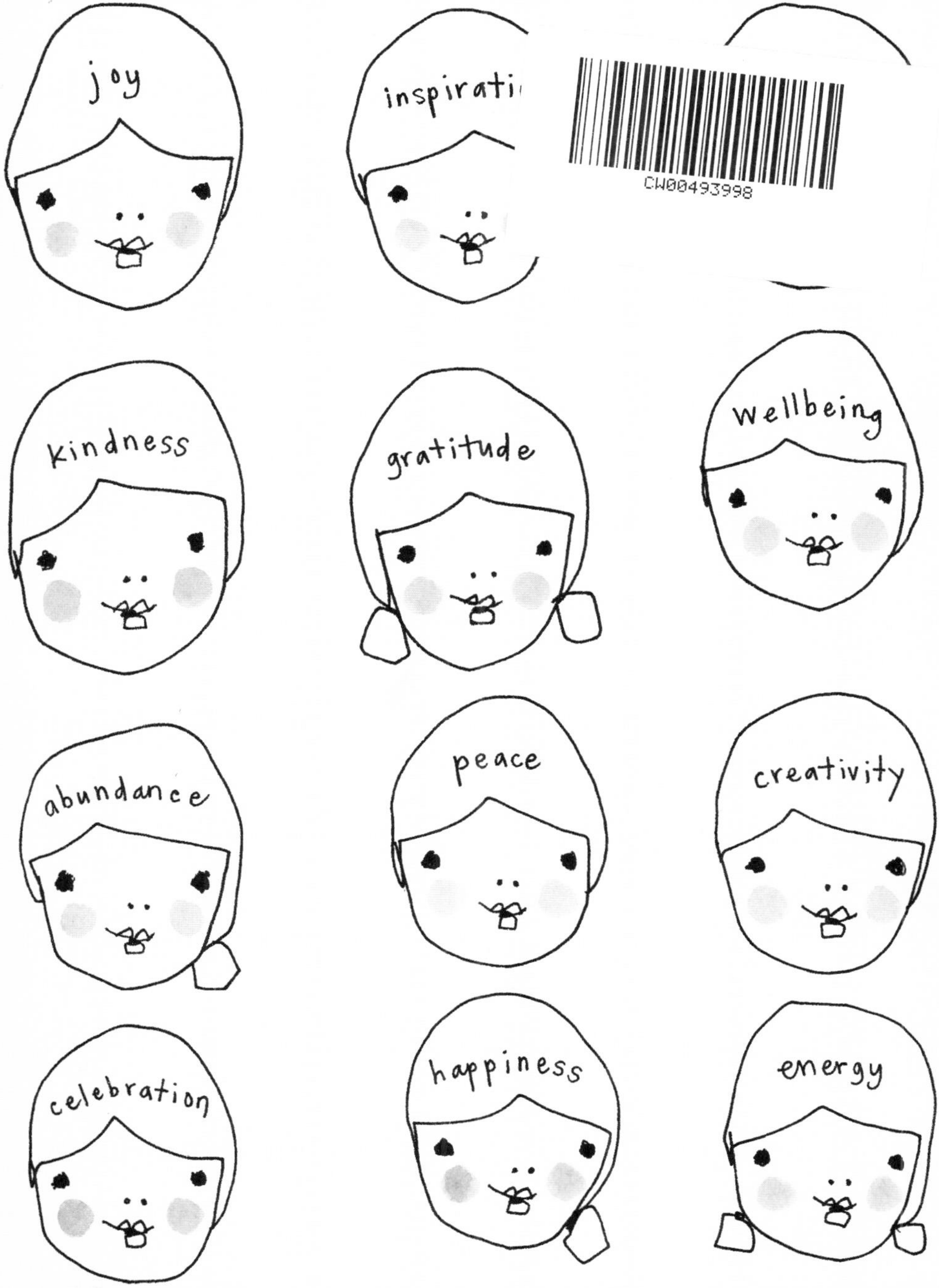
joy
inspirati
kindness
gratitude
wellbeing
abundance
peace
creativity
celebration
happiness
energy

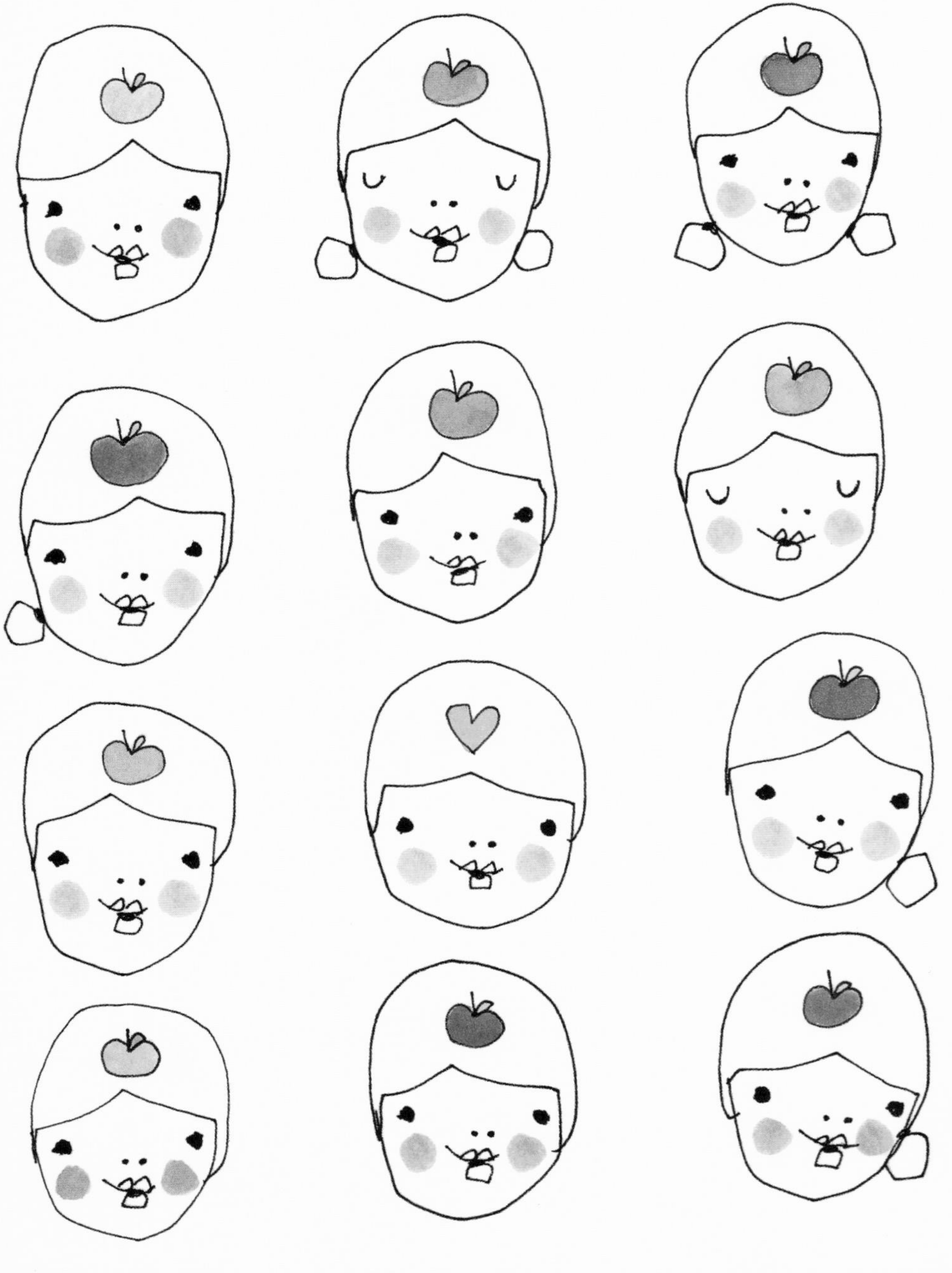

EX LIBRIS

This book belongs to:

THE ART OF GRATITUDE

Meredith Gaston

TABLE OF CONTENTS

3. GRATITUDE AND WELLBEING

Exploring links between gratitude and good health.

4. GRATITUDE AND RELATIONSHIPS

Enhancing, nourishing and transforming relationships through gratitude.

5. GRATITUDE AND ABUNDANCE

Gratitude as the key to abundance. Getting 'in the flow' of life.

6. GRATITUDE AND PRIORITIES

How gratitude helps us to clearly define our real wants and needs.

7. GRATITUDE AND STRESS RELIEF - On the relaxing benefits of being grateful.

»

DEAREST YOU,

I am so pleased that you are holding this little book in your hands. It was meant for you and is ready to change your life. Please use its pages to inspire, guide and nourish you. Try the exercises, fill in the blanks, and explore the words and pictures in your very own way.

This book is a celebration of gratitude and its immense power in daily life. In my eyes, gratitude is the key to happiness, and by cultivating it in daily life, we actually **choose** happiness. Yes! We do have the power to choose!

When we realise this, we can truly take responsibility for designing our own lives.

Our thoughts create our worlds. Positive, uplifting thoughts create inspiring, delightful lives while negative thoughts create and foster negative, lacklustre experiences. Does this sound too simplistic? It **really works!** We need not complicate our lives and create stressful, unpleasant or negative situations for ourselves and others. Being grateful for all we are and all we have is something we choose to do. It is the most powerful, peaceful and joyous way forward in every moment, and it allows all elements of our lives including our health, relationships and environments to take their perfect shape.

Gratitude shapes and binds healthy relationships, nurtures our physical and mental wellbeing, and enhances each and every aspect of being alive. Gratitude truly is life changing.

This little book is organised into colour-coded sections so it's easy to use and enjoy. You might like to read it cover to cover, or dip into the areas that interest you the most in different moments. More than anything I hope you will enjoy yourself, and that these pages will inspire you to travel the grateful path forever more.

I'll **see you there!**

Much love, Meredith xx

♥ COLOUR KEY

You will notice that each section of this book has its own colour from pink to green, orange, purple and blue! Just look for the little ♡ hearts at the foot of each page!

- ♡ Self love
- ♡ Wellbeing
- ♡ Relationships
- ♡ Abundance
- ♡ Priorities
- ♡ Stress Relief
- ♡ Affirmations
- ♡ Sustainable happiness

WHAT IS GRATITUDE ?

Gratitude is officially defined as the quality of being thankful; a readiness to show appreciation for and to return kindness. In my eyes, gratitude is a way of life.

The art of gratitude is about loving life and living in joyous acknowledgement of ourselves, each other and our world. Living gratefully allows us to draw strength and inspiration from all the riches, pleasures and possibilities in our daily lives and multiplies our joy. Gratitude supports and energises our minds and bodies as we live our dreams, and it helps us to gain valuable perspective in any moment.

We create our realities with our thoughts. When we focus on what we lack, we have never seem to have enough. By focusing on what we do have, however, our cup is forever full to overflowing. When we choose gratitude, the endless love, contentment and peace we seek becomes ours to enjoy. Gratitude is not only thankfulness, it is the open door to abundance.

If we take a moment to look around and within, we notice so much to be grateful for. We can be grateful for our very existence, which alone affords us infinite gifts and opportunities. We can simply be with our breathing and experience a miracle! From appreciating a cup of tea or hug from a loved one to admiring a splendrous starry sky, living gratefully, we live fully.

What does gratitude mean to you?

I AM GRATEFUL FOR:

I AM GRATEFUL BECAUSE:

GRATITUDE MAKES ME FEEL:

WHY GRATITUDE ?

Gratitude feels good and is one of the healthiest, most transformative commitments we can make to life, ourselves and each other.

Gratitude is a celebration of life that shapes and fortifies us physically, mentally and emotionally. When we are grateful for our physical bodies and the beauty of our planet, we are inspired to nourish ourselves mindfully and live as well as we possibly can. We appreciate and enjoy nature, we exercise our bodies and we eat natural foods. We flourish in our work and relationships, we remember to rest, and we make time for the things we love. Quite simply, we live mindfully – moment to moment.

When we are grateful for all our joints, our cells, our heartbeats, our breathing and all the wonderful things our bodies can do, from singing and dancing to stretching, growing, seeing, feeling and even creating new life, we honour and energise ourselves. Respect for our bodies and daily positive reinforcement of their beauty and ability make for amazing and sustainable health benefits including increased energy and immunity, excellent mental health, and a dramatically increased sense of overall wellbeing. When we live in gratitude, we are in tune with nature. We notice and care for our planet in supportive ways as we love and notice ourselves more deeply and fully.

Another wonderful aspect of gratitude is that it recognises and grows love. When we as receivers express our gratitude, we make the giving person happy too and thus we double the joy! If you are the recipient of something thoughtful, precious or wonderful, let it be known how thankful you feel, even if it is a simple, everyday thing like a kiss from a loved one or a call from a friend who is thinking of you. Express gratitude and you will multiply the loving energy. More loving energy in circulation will create a more loving world.

Life is full, balanced and complete in light and darkness, day and night, all the four seasons, laughter, tears, stillness and growth. Through it all, we are all entitled to feel satisfied, inspired and deeply rich. Gratitude gives us perspective and helps us to see with positivity in every moment, enhancing our life experience.

Gratitude creates abundance. In the words of Arthur Rubinstein, 'Love life and life will love you back'. When we are grateful for what we have, we invite more good into our lives. What better reason to walk the grateful path? So much joy awaits us!

Last but not least, gratitude is motivating. It allows us to feel deeply satisfied with and inspired by all we have now while encouraging us to recognise our full potential through tomorrow and beyond.

You might like to use the following prompts to explore yourself. What inspires and nurtures you? What makes you happy? Reading over your responses, you will begin to see a clear recipe for happiness in your own life.

THINGS THAT MAKE ME HAPPY:

THINGS THAT INSPIRE ME:

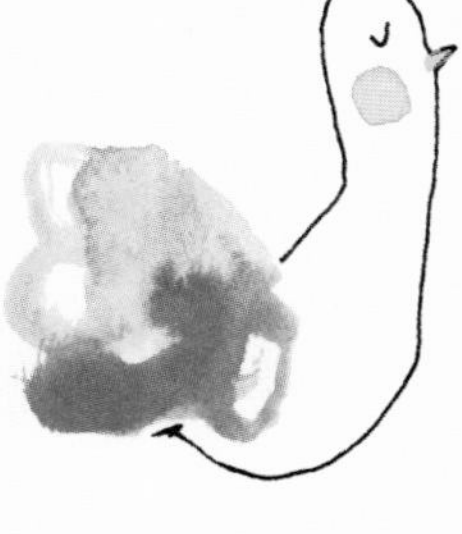

THINGS THAT NURTURE ME:

CHOOSING GRATITUDE

I see gratitude as a way of life available to each one of us in every moment. Consciously choosing gratitude in daily life is an act of love and kindness to ourselves and to each other. We can choose to be grateful and invite more growth, learning, love and abundance into our lives. It is powerful to remember that simple things we take for granted are another person's dream. In every moment, we have the power to choose gratitude and live life richly.

Any negative experience can be seen with fresh eyes if we watch it as a source of learning, or an opportunity to learn, grow and change. We are always presented with challenges at the perfect moments for us to look more deeply within ourselves, connect, heal and grow. Moreover, any positive experience can be lived and breathed to the utmost by being appreciated deeply in the moment.

Shaping our thoughts is something we can all do, and this little book is filled with inspirations and ideas to guide us. Use the prompts below to create a list of features in your ideal life. Reaffirm daily the life you want to live. See it, feel it. Believe it. Commit to it. Draw it, write about it, create it. In doing so, you will live it.

Actively shaping your life

FEELINGS I WANT MORE OF IN MY LIFE:

THOUGHTS I WANT MORE OF IN MY LIFE:

EXPERIENCES I WANT MORE OF IN MY LIFE:

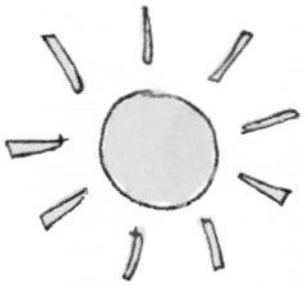

WAYS IN WHICH I EXPRESS MY GRATITUDE:

WAYS I CAN INVITE MORE JOY IN:

CULTIVATING GRATITUDE IN DAILY LIFE

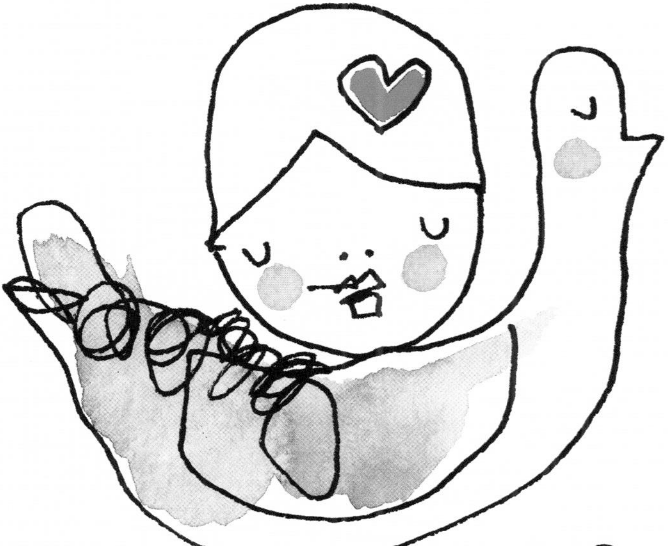

TOP 10 TIPS

TEN TOP TIPS 10

Listed below are ten simple and achievable ways to cultivate gratitude in daily life. Each tip is explored more fully throughout the following chapters with exercises, notes and suggestions to inspire your own sense of gratitude and refresh your commitment to living an amazing life.

1. Begin and end each day with gratitude.

By beginning and ending each day with gratitude we refresh our commitment to living amazing, happy and healthy lives. Keeping a gratitude journal (page 104) is a simple and effective way to harness the power of gratitude in daily life and invite even more joy in! Using simple morning and evening affirmations may also help you to greet and close the day in a revitalising, inspiring and supportive way (page 156).

2. Choose happiness (Yes! It's a choice!)

We choose our thoughts, and in doing so, we create our own realities. Choose happiness and you will live a happy life. Does this sound too simple? It really works! What you give out, you will receive. What you choose to concentrate on will be your focus. Make this work for you by living consciously in gratitude and love.

3. Slow down

Being able to smell the proverbial roses means we need to stop for a moment, inhale and exhale! Slowing down our racing thoughts and agendas is a gift to ourselves and to those we love. It does not mean our productivity need decrease. Quite the contrary! We function so much more effectively when we allow ourselves time to rest, reflect, soak up and appreciate ourselves and all the goodness life brings.

Modern life often champions speed. This was not always the way of the world. Creativity and inspiration are often found in the moments in between. Wandering and daydreaming are fine examples of in between moments and are to be encouraged. When I lived in the mountains, I lived quietly and slowly enough to notice and appreciate all the big and small parts of my day for the first time in my life. From a slow-cooked meal to a beautiful smile, a spontaneous birdsong to a wonderful, meaningful conversation. Living this way, I learnt to be happy.

4. Say thank you to yourself and others and really mean it

Thank you has become a very easy thing to say but really meaning it is something else. Being truly grateful for ourselves, life and the world around us means being in the moment and really feeling the rush of endorphins gratitude sends right through our entire beings. Like love, gratitude blesses us two-fold. The experience, person or thing for which we are thankful is our first gift, our gratitude is another layer upon that, blessing us with even more abundance and more joy. Expressing our gratitude for life, ourselves and each other in meaningful ways makes for immensely rich and life-affirming experiences. We can make ourselves and each other so happy every day in simple, achievable ways. For much more, visit section three on gratitude and relationships.

5. Reinforce your life vision and purpose daily

The art of gratitude is a pleasure to practise and reinforcing it each day strengthens its positive impact on our lives. Vision boards are a great way to keep on track as we visualise and create the lives we dream of (page 110) in addition to journalling (page 104) and daily affirmations (page 156). Other excellent ways to reinforce your life vision and purpose daily is to do things you love and enjoy doing, and to surround yourself with like-minded, feel-good people. Happy, grateful people uplift and inspire us, mirroring our respect for and appreciation of life. As like attracts like, the more in tune we become with our own gratitude and happiness, the happier and more appreciative those around us will be.

6. Write and practise daily affirmations

Few things have been so transformative in my life as the practice of daily affirmations. These powerful statements of truth express and reinforce who we are and what we want in life. The practice of repeating these statements through spoken or written word, repeating them in the mirror, through song, or in any way we possibly can, is an incredibly simple yet effective way of cultivating gratitude and happiness in daily life. By repeating positive statements over and over again, they become ingrained in our subconscious minds and turn into deeply accepted truths. Affirmations do work. See page 156 to get as excited about them as I am! We have so much to gain.

7. Live mindfully

Mindfulness is about really being in our present moment and feeling it. We spend so much time on automatic pilot or in busy-busy thinking mode, that feeling mode is too often switched off. We miss moments of beauty and delicacy in our everyday lives, overlook quieter yet critical signs and messages we should try to catch, and live disengaged from ourselves, others and the world around us.

Focusing on our various electronic devices more often than not disconnects us from the moment, this moment, here and now, the only moment we actually have. The past is gone and the future is not yet here. So living this moment, fully present in it, is all we actually have.

Mindfulness meditation encourages an awareness of our breath as an anchor point for self-awareness. Once I learnt mindfulness meditation techniques I felt my approach to life transform. I made sensitive and thoughtful connections for myself about my life and priorities.

I felt deeply thankful for my mind and body and for the experience of being alive. I also learnt to relax – something I never knew quite how to do. There are some excellent books and recordings for us to share in the Recommended Resources section at the back of this book. Keeping a gratitude journal (page 104) or practising gentle mindfulness meditation exercises (see pages 70 and 130) are both wonderful ways to learn and cultivate the immense power of gratitude in daily life.

8. Connect daily with nature

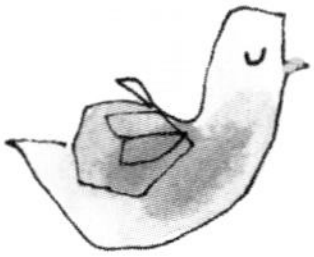

Connecting with nature is a deeply enriching experience and puts life into perspective. Connecting daily with nature by walking, swimming, gardening, riding, hiking, flying or sailing in the outside world is essential for our mental and physical wellbeing. Feel the sun, the wind, the rain and the earth under your feet. Dip your feet in the water. Really look at a tree. Touch its trunk, admire its leaves. Notice the little creatures at your feet or up in the branches. We are part of nature, and we can choose to blend deeply with her rhythms and ways.

Indeed, nature teaches us about life and change through the seasons. Beauty through creatures great and small, colourful flowers, brilliant sunsets, shifting clouds, twinkling stars and humbling mountain ranges. Nature teaches

us patience as seeds turn to vegetables, fruits and flowers. Nature teaches us resilience and trust as it regenerates and renews itself over and over again. Spot that rainbow. Observe that tiny beetle. Linger longer with that view. Look into your pet's eyes. Notice the details.

When travelling, keep a journal and jot down your observations. Become an explorer of the world by appreciating its beauty, uniqueness, ever-newness and splendour. Buddhist monk Thich Nhat Hanh suggests that we walk as if kissing the earth with our feet.

9. Create a beautiful world around you

Our environments say so much about us and they reflect our inner natures, dreams and ideals. Creating beautiful environments in which to live and work uplifts and inspires us, and constantly connects us to our higher selves – our divine happiness. Love and respect your spaces both at home and at work. Keep them neat and clean, choose pictures and objects that move and inspire you. Choose colours that reflect and uplift you. Create a sanctuary at home where you can rest, restore and just be. I love white bed linen and flowers. I love big windows, beautiful ceramics and pieces of furniture with personality. In my studio I love my pencils sharpened and ready in my favourite jar, and I clear my desk at the end of each day.

This way I return to work in the morning feeling refreshed and ready to create anew. These little things have an impact on my life in the biggest ways and I know they will do the same for you!

10. Love yourself

I used to hear the words 'love yourself' and think straight away about my ego and my pride. I thought the idea of loving myself was outlandish, vain and inappropriate. I now hear those words and know they are the key to pure, lifelong happiness.

Loving ourselves has nothing to do with vanity. Loving ourselves is about being deeply grateful for who we are and all we can be. It is about being kind to ourselves in every moment – about choosing praise of ourselves over criticism, and about seeing ourselves as good people, doing our very best, in every given moment. So drop all criticism, regret and comparison. Catch that negative, doubtful little voice when it pipes up in your mind, greet it, thank it for coming, and choose happiness instead. Choose positivity, confidence and self-support. Love yourself so much that you truly know and understand your self-worth. This love you have for yourself will transform your life in ways you will never even believe. It is the most powerful force there is, beyond words or definition, and it is at your fingertips now and forever.

GRATITUDE and SELF LOVE

BE
YOU
TIFUL.

☆ BeYOUtiful ☆

The way we walk, the way we talk, the way we think, the way we dress, the way we sing, dance, solve problems and love each other is as diverse and varied as our DNA. The things that make us different are the things that make us lovable, unique and unforgettable. By being grateful for and living out our uniqueness, we learn to love ourselves.

Each day is a new opportunity for us to explore our creativity; to celebrate life. By thinking independently we become original, authentic and interesting people. Really be-ing ourselves is the most wonderful, fun and essential part of being alive.

Despite ideologies of all kinds, the liberating epiphany is: there is no such thing as 'normal'. There is no universally agreed correct way to live, nor is there a normal way to look or to feel. As the beautiful old Chinese proverb goes, 'Tension is what you think you should be, relaxation is who you are.' Relaxation is essential to our wellbeing and our enjoyment of life. When you feel comfortable, notice that feeling. That is you. You are a genuine 'one-off', a once-in-a-lifetime being in this big wide world. It really doesn't get any more special than that.

TO LOVE
ONESELF IS
THE BEGINNING
OF A LIFELONG
ROMANCE.

Oscar Wilde ♥

DARE TO BE DIFFERENT

Not only are we all different, we are constantly changing. Life ensures that we are different beings in a different world from day to day.

As living things, we are affected by processes of endless change. We are affected by time, gravity, seasons and experiences of all kinds. Our preferences, tastes and self-expressions change too, from pleasures such as favourite foods, clothes, music and art, to our social lives, hobbies, romances and friendships. We just need to look back at certain outfits we wore, thoughts we thought, words we said or things we did then – things that may make us laugh, cringe or cry now!

We must honour ourselves by staying in tune with our changing needs. We are unique, flexible beings with endless reservoirs of creativity. The many adventures we live stitch squares in the magnificent patchworks of our lives. In our patchworks, every piece and every stitch counts. Showing ourselves the kindness and gratitude we deserve as we walk our paths allows us to make sense of life and appreciate ourselves in the face of change.

Indeed, the energy of change surrounding us creates an atmosphere ripe for personal transformation and filled with endless possibilities. When we live with eyes and hearts open, we are constantly learning and growing. We flourish. Living in constant flux may feel confronting at times, yet we needn't feel overwhelmed. We are safe in change when we live mindfully, love ourselves and trust in life. We can let go, knowing that we are always changing for the better and deepening more and more comfortably into ourselves as we go.

YOUR HEART
IS AS **DEEP**
AS AN OCEAN.

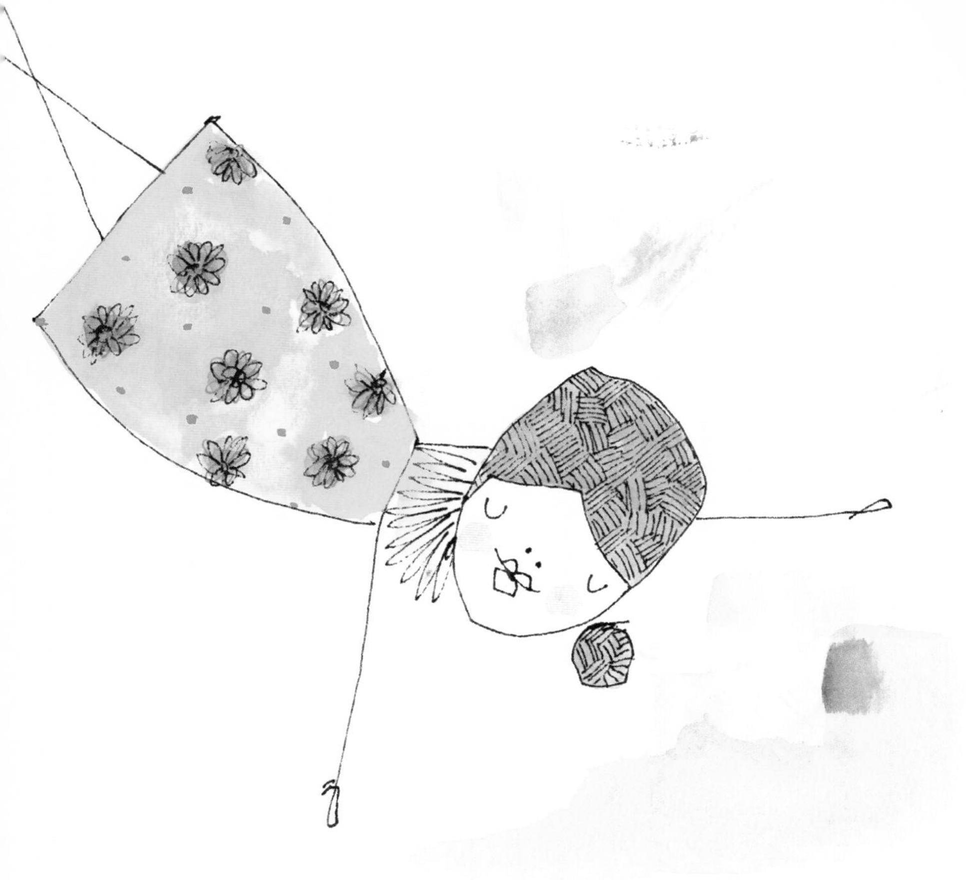

GO FIND YOURSELF
IN ITS HIDDEN DEPTHS.

—Rumi—

COMPARISON

Richer, righter, bigger, better? In the words popularly attributed to Theodore Roosevelt, 'Comparison is the thief of joy.'

We too easily measure ourselves, our achievements or our circumstances against others' in order to gauge our success or assess our worth. Our own happiness is far deeper and more personal than anybody else's reality, experience or opinion.

By letting go of the tendency to constantly compare ourselves to others, we may live fully and joyously at last. We can bring to an end the self-sabotaging cycle of unhappiness that we too often perpetuate, albeit subconsciously. Live with respect for yourself and others. Allow bountiful praise, gratitude and laughter to replace life-limiting comparison and watch yourself blossom!

WHAT I'M
LOOKING FOR
IS NOT OUT THERE,
IT IS IN ME. ♡

Helen Keller

It is easy to live
for others; everybody
does.
I call on you to live
for yourselves.

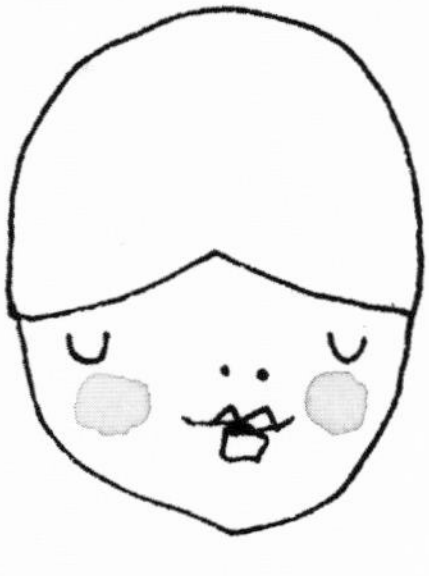

Ralph Waldo Emerson

PERFECTION

There is a beautiful concept in Japanese creative philosophy known as wabi-sabi. It suggests that it is the unexpected, natural, or imperfect characteristics of an object that make it special. The same can be said for us as human beings! Constantly striving for perfection is too often at the expense of our happiness, relaxation and enjoyment. It also encourages much self-criticism and deprecation, habits well worth breaking for good.

Just like beauty, perfection is completely subjective and in the eye of the beholder. Sometimes we are so caught up in 'perfecting' ourselves and our work to our own self-set standards that we miss the natural beauty within and around us. We miss how well we are actually doing at life. Stifling perfectionism takes away our capacity for relaxation and enjoyment. It is essential that we aim high in life, with self-love, not self-criticism.

We are all learning, building and growing. Next time try constructive awareness rather than constructive criticism when considering your personal development. Be aware of how well you are doing and congratulate yourself. When you identify room for improvement, positively affirm your ability to make the necessary changes and be grateful in advance for the divine assistance you will receive in achieving your goals. Your more positive, constructive outlook will work wonders for you.

Perfection is lived as an experience or a feeling. Often the most beautiful memories, magic moments or captivating people are unforgettable for the most unexpected, imperfect reasons. Let's allow room for ourselves to just revel in the way we are, true *wabi-sabi* style, each and every new day.

ABOVE ALL
DO NOT FORGET
YOUR DUTY
TO LOVE YOURSELF.

Søren Kierkegaard

THE THINGS THAT MAKE ME DIFFERENT

I AM INSPIRED BY

THINGS THAT WARM MY HEART

THINGS THAT MAKE ME CURIOUS

THINGS THAT MAKE ME LAUGH

QUALITIES I POSSESS THAT I ADMIRE

QUALITIES I ADMIRE IN OTHERS

TO ME, PERFECTION MEANS

NOTHING
CAN BRING YOU
PEACE
BUT
YOURSELF.

Ralph Waldo Emerson

GRATITUDE and WELLBEING

CHOOSING GRATITUDE FOR GOOD HEALTH

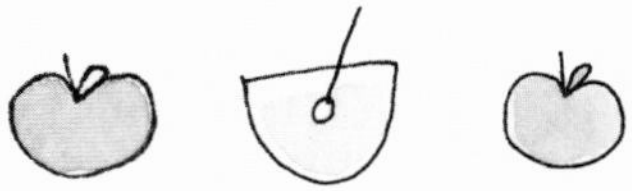

Our bodies' cells work best in happy, positive environments. The energy of our thoughts is circulated through our entire system. This means every cell, organ and gland 'feels' with us. Our thoughts are experienced by our bodies as a whole in every moment. If you question this truth, simply consider blushing, spontaneous laughter, butterflies in the stomach, nervous twitches, or free-flowing tears! These involuntary physical signs demonstrate that our whole bodies actually 'feel' with our minds.

Positive and negative thoughts and feelings affect us respectively in physical ways. Like love, gratitude is experienced as a positive vibration in our bodies. Its frequency is both light and deep, joyous and blissful. Feeling gratitude for something or someone makes for double the joy as gratitude in itself blesses us again.

In my eyes, living gratefully is the key to happiness in daily life. As Aristotle famously pointed out, choosing to be happy is good for our health. This simple statement captures so much, especially the idea of 'choice' and the possibility of 'choosing' to be happy.

Indeed, as neuroscience increasingly shows, our minds are 'plastic', flexible, and open to training. Neuroplasticity describes the science of assessing how our minds can learn, develop and change, and how our bodies are responsive to these changes. By choosing happiness and gratitude, we are giving our cells the very best environment in which to thrive. Through consistently drawing on positive thoughts and affirmations, we can empower ourselves, literally choosing happiness and health as our way of life. For a more in-depth passage on the concept of choosing happiness, see page 174.

H2O

THE FIRST WEALTH IS HEALTH

Ralph Waldo Emerson

WELLNESS BY MOTHER NATURE:

SUNSHINE

WATER

REST

AIR

MOVEMENT

NOURISHMENT

PEACE

- Meredith -

CELEBRATION (Not Deprivation!)

Strict diets and intensive exercise regimes can feel like punishment to our minds and bodies and more often than not, they are. Living a happy and healthy life is not about deprivation, competition and struggle, it is about balance, self-love and self-respect.

Negative mental patterns surrounding food and exercise can be transformed with an attitude of gratitude – a celebration of our minds, our bodies and our lives. Next time you eat, really connect with and appreciate your food. Be grateful for its freshness, its colour, its flavour and the nourishment it provides. Be thankful for the bountiful options you have when choosing seasonal produce to cook with and enjoy. Think about the excitement of trying something new, experiencing another culture through food, or sampling divine earthly delights such as a just-picked apple, a ripe mulberry or a fresh fig. Prepare healthful home-cooked meals made with love. Pour love and gratitude into your cooking, and the food will taste amazing. It will even give love to those with whom you share it!

When we love and appreciate ourselves, we naturally want to look after ourselves as best as we can. Choosing natural foods is an act of love for ourselves. When we love ourselves, we eat just as much as we need – neither too little nor too much. We learn to listen to ourselves and find our own perfect balance. Our bodies are precious and sacred and deserve our loving care and attention. Indulge yourself naturally, be it with regular massages, baths, manicures or aromatherapy. Take the time to eat well, choose natural personal care products, and drink plenty of filtered water to stay hydrated throughout the day. By taking care with what we put into our bodies and on to our skins we are honouring ourselves. We are living, breathing beings and we function best when keeping it real.

Overly rigorous exercise routines can also make us feel poorly. While challenging ourselves is essential to our personal growth and development, this can be done without the internal warfare. Love your body into beauty by exercising it in ways you love and enjoy. Rather than burn yourself out, uplift yourself. Be flexible with your outlook and approach as your needs change day to day, season to season. Whenever possible, get outdoors and into nature. This will further amp up the feel-good factor. I love bush or beach walks so much because I am inspired by the beauty of the scenery as I go. Most importantly, listen to your body and be kind. Always.

It has been said
that life has treated
me harshly; and
sometimes I have
complained in my heart
because many pleasures
of human experience
have been withheld from
me... if much has been
denied me, much, very much,
has been given me...

Inspired by

Helen Keller

(who was both deaf
and blind)

SPEAKING BODY

Learning to listen to our bodies and our instincts means possessing the key to our health and wellbeing. Our body's wisdom (or our inner wisdom) is our most powerful tool. It caters to our individuality, grasps our shifting needs in any given moment, and guides us to look after ourselves in the best way possible. In its immediacy and honesty, our bodies' wisdom is never wrong.

Instinct and body wisdom, arguably one and the same, are like muscles. The more you use them, the stronger, more trustworthy and more useful they become. Exercise your body's wisdom by listening to your 'gut instinct' – the immediate responses that come to you before over-thinking. Trust your body's wisdom to guide you into only good energy situations, protect you from harm or discomfort, encourage you to explore things that serve you on a soul level, and stimulate your heart.

In the quieter days before mobile phones and tablets, mp3 players and social media, people had time and space to listen to themselves without interruption and develop their senses. For many of us, we need to actively and consciously take time out to work with these innate skills. Mindfulness meditation, yoga, journalling and time in nature are essential. They are not complicated to practise, can cater to all body types, and they build our connection with our inner wisdom.

THINGS I CURRENTLY DO TO NURTURE MY HEALTH AND WELLBEING

THE THINGS I LOVE AND APPRECIATE ABOUT MY BODY

MY IDEA OF WELLNESS IS

3 WAYS I CAN POSITIVELY IMPACT MY OWN WELLNESS JOURNEY NOW

1 ____________ 2 ____________ 3 ____________

SOME PEOPLE
GRUMBLE
THAT ROSES
HAVE THORNS;

I AM GRATEFUL
THAT THORNS
HAVE
ROSES.

Kahlil Gibran

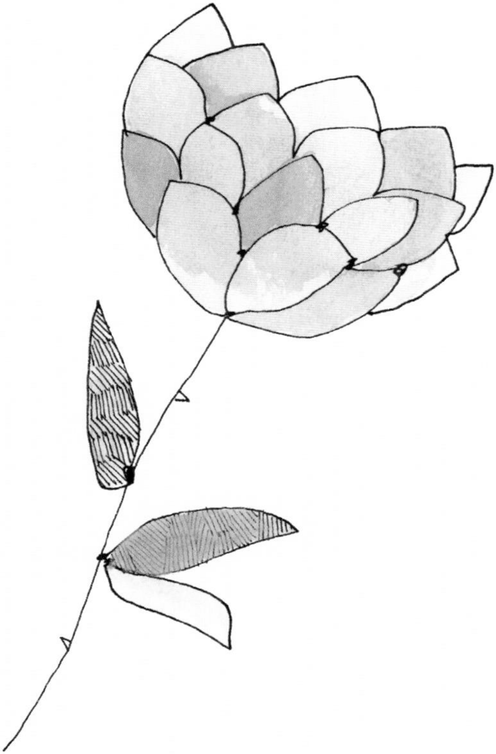

GRATITUDE AND HEALING

We all possess our very own unique, naturally miraculous, intelligent and self-healing power. Our minds and bodies work together constantly with us and for us – wanting us to be radiantly healthy, happy and whole. Nietzsche famously suggested that there is more wisdom in our bodies than in the deepest philosophies.

Have you ever stopped to be grateful for your body, for your eyes that see? For your hands that touch and feel? For your feet that have taken you so many places? For your heart that beats and circulates blood and energy throughout your body? For your breathing that provides your cells with oxygen, and refreshes and detoxifies your system? Thank your body daily and you will be amazed at how happy it makes you feel.

More often than not, the parts of our bodies that are crying out for our love and attention are the ones that need our gratitude the most. Pain and discomfort carry their very own personal messages, especially for us. While it is easy to be frustrated when we feel we are not working 'perfectly' in a particular area or way and then damn that area, it is even more critical to bless that part of ourselves with love and connect with the message it brings.

One way I have found to do this is via body scan meditations. Connecting with each part of our bodies as we go, we have a chance to acknowledge and be grateful for all the essential parts of ourselves. There are many tapes that can guide you through a progressive body relaxation meditation, though the basics are on page 70 for you.

Before your meditation, ask healing energy to reach each part of your body (or a person) you are thinking of and that needs your TLC. Some people may call this art 'prayer'. No matter what, we are essentially using the loving energy of our minds and hearts to encourage and bring about positive change and healing for ourselves, not to mention others and the world we live in.

BODY SCAN MEDITATION

Relax, soothe, energise, connect.

I love to take time out to do this body scan meditation as often as possible because it is so therapeutic and relaxing. It is also a really powerful way to connect with yourself and appreciate all the wonderful parts of your living, breathing body. I like to lie down on my yoga mat or on my bed, but if you feel more comfortable seated, this will work beautifully too.

Simply close your eyes and bring your attention to your breathing. You might like to place your hands lightly over your abdomen and follow the rise and fall of your breathing. We spend so much time breathing in a shallow way, yet when we practise deep breathing from our bellies we really allow for deeper wellbeing – we oxygenate our cells and 'breathe' our whole body. Breathe on for a minute or so and notice how much calmer you already feel.

Next take your attention to your toes, when you are ready, and just notice them. How do they feel? You may have never 'felt' your toes before, so this may be an interesting experience. You don't need to 'think' about your toes, just 'feel' them. Next gently move to the soles of your feet. How do they feel? Breathe into them. Your soles have been so many places. They are such important parts of you. Next move to your ankles and be with them. What do they feel like? Continue to your legs. Feel your shins and calves, your knees and thighs, feel their length and their solidity, their strength and their energy. You might feel a buzzing in your knees, a pain here or there, just breathe into it. Your legs are so wonderful. Take a breath to acknowledge them.

Continue on through your entire body in this thoughtful way. Your abdomen, chest, lungs and heart, your arms, hands and fingers, the amazing palms of your hands... think of all the things your hands allow you to create, experience and feel and just BE with them. Next visit your neck and shoulders, your upper and lower back, and release any tension held in these areas. Consciously let go of the tension and double confirm the letting go with a few deep breaths.

By now you are likely to be feeling light and floaty. Your deep breathing will be flowing and all the cells in your body breathing with you. Take a moment to notice the rhythym created by your in-breath and your out-breath, the rise of your belly then the fall, the gentle air releasing as you breathe out your nostrils. This is being alive... Breath is our life force!

Move to your face and feel your eyes, your nose and your mouth. How do they feel? What about your jaw, your teeth, your gums and your lips? Each day we use our faces to speak, to see, to smell, and to hear. We smile, we talk with our eyes, we cry, we sing, we do and say so many things. Feel the muscles in your face. Where there is any tension, especially around the jaw and temples, just release this tightness and breathe deeply, as if you were breathing up from under your face. Let your skin

breathe and relax. Feel your ears, inside and out. Can you sense any pressure? Hear any noise? Just notice your ears. Thank them as you breathe with them.

Lastly, move to your head as a whole and feel it. Notice its weight, its shape... how does it feel? Breathe into the area at the very base of your skull, and into the top of your head. What does the space around your head feel like? Breathe into your whole head as if you are opening a window, letting fresh, cleansing air move through it. If any areas or points of discomfort rise to your attention, just breathe with them and let them go.

As you are lying (or sitting) in the peaceful, relaxed state you have lovingly created for yourself, take a few final deep breaths down through the top of your head, right through the soles of your feet. Do this and feel your breath pass through the entire length of your body. What a wonderful feeling. When you are ready, gently open your eyes. ★

And when you crush
an apple with your teeth,
say to it in your heart:

Your seeds shall live in
my body,
And the buds of your
tomorrow shall blossom
in my heart,
And your fragrance shall
be my breath,
And together we will
rejoice,
through all the seasons.

– Attributed to Kahlil Gibran –

GRATITUDE and RELATIONSHIPS

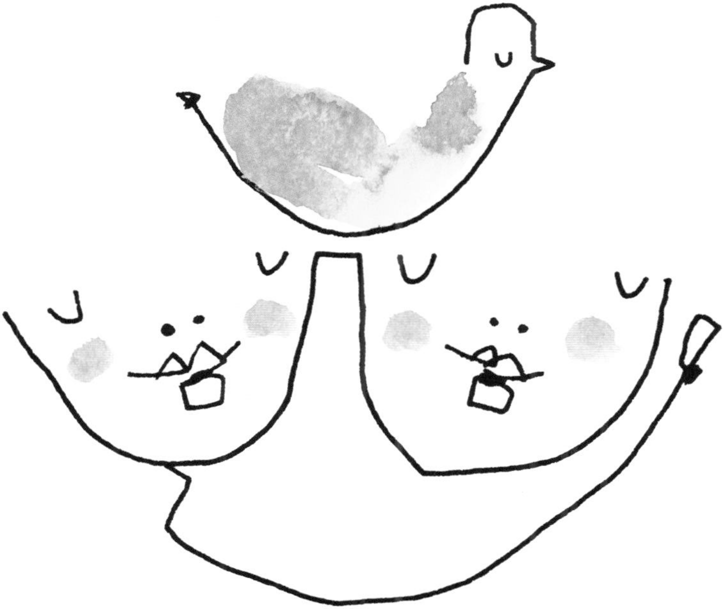

EXPRESSING GRATITUDE

We all know how good it feels to receive a gift, a compliment, a letter, or special attention from people we care about in our lives. For many of us, it is just as much a joy to give these things as to receive them. When I make or find a gift for somebody I love, I often can't wait to give it to them! It's almost like I'm the one getting the present by giving it. And moreover, it is just so simple to do.

When we give compliments to others, we show them our appreciation and we strengthen them deeply. By recognising and appreciating others, we allow them to recognise and appreciate themselves. Research shows that managers who remember to say 'thank you' to their staff may find that those employees feel motivated to work harder. Partners who took time to express gratitude for each other not only felt more positive toward the other person but also felt more comfortable expressing concerns about their relationship. The circulation of gratitude is truly powerful!

It is equally important for us to receive gifts and praise with grace. When we are given a compliment, it is vital for us to accept it with grace too, rather than directly deflecting or rejecting it. When we are being complimented, the most wonderful way for us to respond is to smile and say thank you. Self-deprecation is deeply discouraging. Your entire being responds to your thinking in every moment, so knowing you deserve happiness, health, peace and abundance means really having and enjoying all of those gifts. The word gratitude is derived from the Latin word *gratia*, meaning grace, or graciousness. There is an infinite amount of love to be shared. Be a part of it!

YOU CAN NEVER
DO A KINDNESS
TOO SOON
BECAUSE YOU
NEVER KNOW HOW
SOON WILL BE
TOO LATE.

— Ralph Waldo Emerson —

EXPRESS YOUR GRATITUDE WITH FLAIR!

The Love Note

This timeless and much appreciated approach to expressing your love and gratitude is about taking a moment to put pen to paper, in the name of love! A perfect way to tell spouses, friends or family members that you love them, the love note needn't be long nor floral (unless you wish it to be!) just a few simple, thoughtful words put your way. We can start by thinking of the special qualities the recipient possesses, or about the things they do to light up our life. There is no better time than now to let those you love know how you feel!

My favourite way with love notes is to tuck them into everyday spots for a little surprise. I pop little notes into my beloved's lunch box, under his pillow or in his morning tea-cup, and I post letters per snail-mail to give something tangible to those I love. It may take that bit longer than electronic mail, but it is a joyous and thoughtful gesture that will make somebody's day and encourage them to think about sharing the love too! ♡

The Thank-you Note

In the olden days, there was a lot more correspondence by hand. The beauty of this was that recipients could touch and feel the words sent to them, and that senders could personalise the presentation of their message in unique ways. Invitations, thank-you notes and latest news updates were penned and shared. Why not be a bit classic and start writing real thank-you notes? You might find beautiful stationery that inspires you, or create your own letterhead! There are so many opportunities to send thank-you notes and with a few little minutes of your time, you really can make somebody's day! It is so nice to be appreciated and so sustaining to be appreciative.

The Flowers

An unexpected floral delivery from an admirer or friend can be just the ticket. Try surprising someone you're thinking of with blooms, even hand-picked from your garden, to share beauty and joy with them and let them know they're loved. Simple, fresh and greatly appreciated.

The Family Letterbox Network

I once visited a friend's home in The Blue Mountains and noticed that each door had a letter bag or pouch attached. I was told that these 'letterboxes' were for internal mail- family correspondence. If there was any kind of special news, or thoughts or feelings that one family member wanted to express to another, they would be able to write to each other as an alternative to spoken words. Things better expressed or more easily shared on paper. The unspoken rule was that all mail is private! The sense of mutual respect and openness was inspiring. If this arrangement might work in your home, why not give it a try!? Have fun making your letterboxes and putting your thoughts into little notes. * NB - It was mentioned to me that while honesty and constructive feedback were ALWAYS welcomed, hurtful or derogatory notes were not allowed. The great news was, my friend explained, there was no cause for these anyway.

The Mix Tape

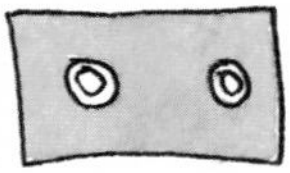

Say it with music! Songs can say so much. The classic approach is the mix tape, a series of dedications to the recipient. People appreciate the thoughtfulness and effort that goes into a mix-tape, and the tailor-made appeal of them means the mixer and the addressee will both understand the significance of the play list. Be a DJ for a day and give this approach a go!

The 'Breaking of Bread'

Food is life! Sharing food, loving food and caring about food in daily life is investing in our wellbeing, nourishment and happiness. You needn't be a masterchef to concoct a love-filled meal. In fact, simple is quite often best. A home-cooked meal with a few thoughtful touches to set the mood from candles to flowers to pretty napkins never fails to delight and impress.

Making meal times special means creating rituals of connecting and BE-ing with each other, not to mention being present to the joyous experience of eating and appreciating all the earthly delights available to us. While couples, friends and families get busy and there is always something to do next, marking out a sacred time of the day to come together around the table, be that breakfast, lunch or dinner, means committing to each other and putting the emphasis on togetherness. Make sure no one is left with all the organising and that tasks are shared. Everyone should be part of creating the magic. This is a very important piece of daily life and presents so many opportunities to cultivate gratitude.

If you live alone, you might like to invite somebody whose company you enjoy to dine with you. They will feel so appreciated by the effort you make, and will very likely feel inclined to return the invitation. Here's to breaking the proverbial bread together!

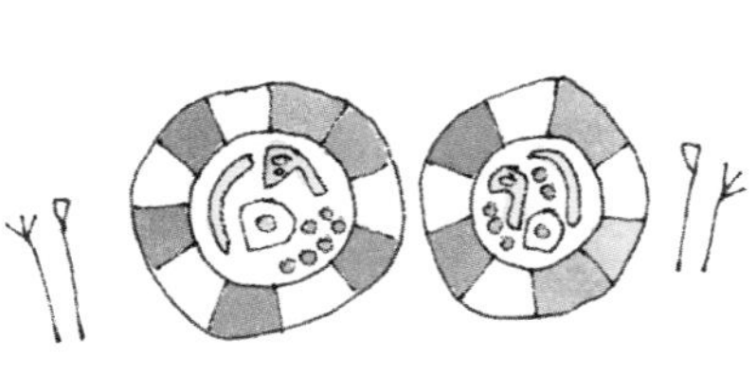

The Care Package

Have you ever wanted to reach out to a loved one during a hard time? Sometimes the right words may be hard to find, or something a bit special and comforting is required. Why not create a little care package and say 'I'm thinking of you'? ♡

You might like to include herbal teas, magazines, body products or gourmet nibbles, anything you know your loved one will really enjoy. You might write a little note or pack everything beautifully and deliver it anonymously to their door! Posting is of course another option. Mail like this is unforgettable.

NONE of these options cost the earth, nor are they complex or time consuming. You can say so much with love, and by making the time to really express yourself, you invite infinite joy into your own life and the lives of others.

Feeling gratitude and not expressing it is like wrapping a present and not giving it!

- Attributed to William Arthur Ward -

CUDDLING AND TOUCH

On the topic of love and connection, let's touch on touch!
Yes, a touch can say a thousand words.

The benefits of affectionate human touch are multiple – and there are some very solid, enlightening scientific explanations as to why it feels so good to get and give cuddles. Oxytocin is a hormone released in the body when we experience touch and intimacy. When we cuddle oxytocin abounds, sending feelings of wellbeing, love and positive energy from our heads to our toes. Cuddling can relieve pain and stress, boost our immunity, and even contribute to the health of our physical hearts! Cuddling is also an expression of love, gratitude and affection being given and received, and can re-energise our self-worth and self-esteem.

Intimacy and physical contact of all kinds are vital to our health and wellbeing. After all, we are primal beings and have a deep, physical need for connection. We only need to look at the tenderness between animals to see how natural and life-affirming physical contact and connection truly are. Try a little extra cuddling this week and allow yourself and those around you to feel the love.

Above and beyond
what you say and do,
people will remember
how you make them feel.

— Inspired by Maya Angelou —

COMMUNITY SPIRIT

Community spirit is a feeling of involvement in and love for one's community. Communities take many shapes from families to workplaces to schools, from local to sporty to artistic and cultural groups.

Community spirit also means lending a helping hand to friends and neighbours, taking part in local activities such as markets, performances and workshops, even volunteering. I experience community spirit in my home town as being grateful for familiar faces, sharing produce together from our gardens, and supporting local businesses and organisations. There are few things more enriching than a sense of belonging.

By making time to be actively involved in our communities, we make time to genuinely connect with others and open ourselves to support, learning and friendship. Health professionals agree that an active social life is crucial for our collective health and wellbeing. Look in your local paper, check in at your local library or council, or browse online for ways to get involved in your community. Feel the mind and body benefits of community spirit in your life.

Some of us are less social than others, but isolating ourselves from activity around us creates loneliness and disconnection. Don't be shy – this life was designed for sharing and there is plenty more love to go around than we will ever know!

We are in the same boat.

– Pope Clement I –

Even after all this
time the sun never
says to the earth
'you owe me'.

Look what happens
with a love like
that, it lights up the
whole sky.

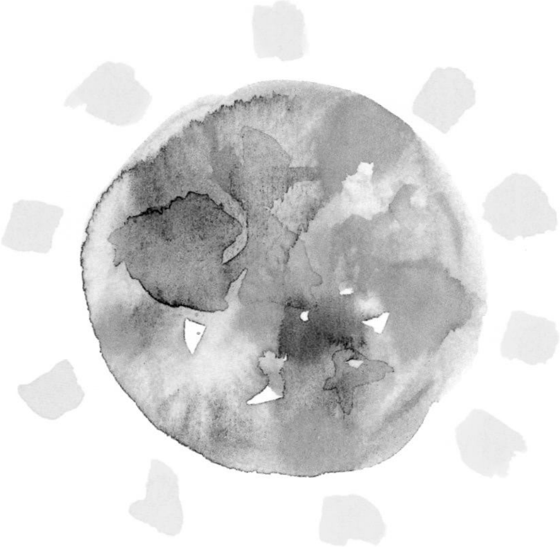

– Attributed to –
Hafez

GRATITUDE and ABUNDANCE

Gratitude can

transform common days
into thanksgivings,
turn routine jobs into joy,
and **change** ordinary opportunities
into blessings.

— Attributed to
William Arthur Ward

ABUNDANCE AWAITS THROUGH GRATITUDE'S OPEN DOOR

The word 'abundance' is a beautiful one – it describes plenty, richness and fullness. It is about having enough (and usually even more!) of what we we need and desire in this life. True abundance is felt rather than bought or owned. Abundance is a way of thinking, a quality of life, and it is possible for all of us to experience, every day.

It is amazing how simply and profoundly we can transform our health with thoughts of abundance and prosperity. Focusing on what we lack or what we feel is 'missing' in our lives attracts lucklustre feelings and experiences. Quite simply, by focusing on what we lack, we never seem to have enough.

By focusing on what we do have and love, however, we actively count our blessings and kickstart a remarkable chain reaction of positive, often unimaginable connections!

Our bodies' natural inclinations are toward perfect health, happiness and abundance. Support your natural health and wellbeing with your positive thoughts, and feel the difference starting today.

'ENERGY FLOWS WHERE ATTENTION GOES'

I love these wise and simple words because they pack a very practical punch! It's as simple as this. When we put our attention on to a subject, feeling or experience, our physical and mental energy flows there. By choosing where we place our attention, we shape our energy. The energy we give and receive shapes the happiness or unhappiness we experience in daily life. Think happiness and you will receive it. Think abundance and it will be yours. This is not esoteric stuff, it is based on the simple, age-old laws of attraction.

As human beings, we need to take responsibility for our energy and life experiences. We cannot wait for miracles to happen, we need to create them.

Here are a couple of examples. By keeping a gratitude journal or Vision Board (page 110) and focusing daily on all the things for which we are grateful, our energy flows into all the things we love. As a result, the things we love and enjoy are magnified, nourished and strengthened. They take our centre stage. In contrast, by focusing on negative emotions and letting our attention hone in on resentment, doubt, fear, disease or dissatisfaction, these experiences and emotions will dominate and even worse, multiply.

If we constantly worry about our finances and our health, for instance, it makes sense that we will more than likely experience financial problems and compromised health. If we focus on our general wealth and the strength of our bodies, no matter our age or capacity, these parts will strengthen, along with others, beyond our wildest expectations. For the parts we want to work on and heal, we can start doing positive affirmations (page 156) or nurturing our wellbeing (page 54). These techniques work.

Try watching how energy flows where your attention goes by practising mindfulness meditation (exercises pages 70, 130, 145–6) and checking in with your body from top to toe. Last but not least, surround yourself with like-mindedly positive people. Share and grow the good energy! Revolutionise your own life. By surrounding yourself with positive, joyous people, your own beliefs will be re-energised and reinforced. In the wise words attributed to Walt Whitman, 'Keep your face toward the sunshine and all shadows will fall behind you.'

'Where you come from' said the little prince 'People grow five thousand roses in one garden, and still they do not find what they are looking for'.

'No, they do not find it' I replied.

'Yet what they are looking for could be found in a single rose or a handful of water'.

'That is True' I replied.

And he added:

'But the eyes are blind. One must see with the heart'.

'The Little Prince', Antoine de Saint-Exupéry.

GRATITUDE JOURNALLING

A delightful byproduct of the grateful way is a remarkable and deeply joyous sense of abundance that begins to fill and shape daily life. Counting our blessings is about really taking time to think about all the good we experience in our lives, and being truly thankful for it.

Even experiences we find uncomfortable or challenging are learning experiences and possess their own transformative power. Gratitude journalling is a way to count our blessings daily, celebrate and shape our lives, and invite even more good in. As per the laws of attraction, like attracts like. Your gratitude will simply bring about more reasons, events and people into your life for you to feel grateful for! It is a life-affirming chain reaction of beauty and goodness that further reinforces our commitment to happiness, health and positivity.

I keep my gratitude journal on my bedside table and I write in it either upon waking or when tucking in at night. Even if that means just a few words. It might even be a list of three things that day for which I felt grateful. Sunshine; a friend's smile; a lovely, unexpected letter. I started gratitude journalling by listing things, drawing things and occasionally writing sentences. I love to take care with my journals but I never strive for neatness or perfection on any page. We should feel free to express ourselves in these pages for ourselves and let our thoughts flow. It is easy to wake up in the morning and reach first for our electronic devices, checking messages, emails or social media for the latest updates. Same goes for bed-time, another sacred time of the day, and an another ideal opportunity to connect with ourselves, reflect on the good in our lives, dream and plan ahead. If instead of reaching for our phones or devices, we light a candle, stretch or write in our journals, we choose to connect more fully with our physical reality rather than immediately zone into another dimension.

Your gratitude journal is a great place for you to write and repeat your affirmations (page 156). The many affirmations I have written in my gratitude journal have become my easy truths, sinking into my subconscious via repetition and creating a happier, healthier daily life for me to savour. Allow your journal to reflect you – add colour, photographs or drawings if you wish, find a pen or pencil you love and a book you enjoy using. In the Recommended Resources section of this book, you will find some inspiring examples of illustrated diaries and books to help you on your way. You will create something personal, beautiful and uplifting to treasure, and your focus on gratitude will change your world. I love every journal I have filled, and when I get to the end of a book, I keep it close by so I can reflect on the way I continue to design and light up my own life.

YOUR OWN GRATITUDE JOURNAL

Making lists of the great things in your life, reflecting on your daily life experiences and inviting even more abundance into your heart is what gratitude journalling is all about! It is simple, fun, relaxing and transformative. Choose a time of day that feels right to you and make putting pen to paper in this way a ritual. The results will amaze you.

Find a little note book and marker you like. Be as neat or as messy as you please. This is your space. You might like to use the prompts below to encourage your stream of consciousness. Collect things, draw, daydream, plan and document your one, amazing life.

THE THINGS I NOTICED:

TODAY'S BEST MOMENT:

THESE THINGS GOT ME EXCITED:

I FELT:

I THOUGHT ABOUT:

I ASK THE UNIVERSE:

TAKE A MOMENT NOW TO JOT DOWN SOME THINGS IN YOUR LIFE FOR WHICH YOU ARE GRATEFUL:

I'M BUSY MAKING THIS DAY WONDERFUL!
Meredith

VISION BOARDS

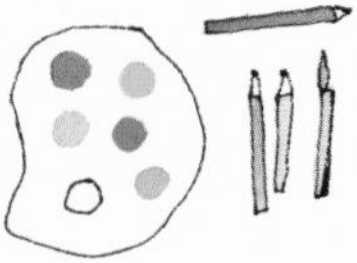

Another active way to manifest a life you love is to make a habit of visualising it. There are many ways to do this including journalling and meditating, but another great way that's both fun and beautiful is creating a vision board.

Simply hang a big board above your desk or bed with lots of space for inspirations. You might choose a cork board or cover some light wood in pretty fabric. Use this space to pin up images that represent and capture what you love. You might draw inspiration from travel, health or beauty magazines, newspapers, cards, textiles, postcards, sketches, notes or photographs. When you come across some words you love, write them down and pin them up on your board too. Soon you will see a personalised montage of beauty and joy in front of you, reinforcing your own vision for a wonderful life and keeping you endlessly focused and inspired.

Our vision boards change and grow as we do so don't be afraid to refresh, adjust, replace or annotate the inspirations you choose. If you feel sentimental about your collection, you might like to keep a special box in which you place them once you're ready to refresh your space. You will then have an exciting and memorable collection of inspirations to treasure, documenting the pictures, words and moments that caught your heart.

Keeping powerful, uplifting visuals at a glance is part of putting our joy, pleasure and gratitude in the limelight of our lives. The simple and joyous practice of keeping a vision board goes a great way towards us manifesting all the daily good we are deeply entitled to celebrate in this life.

familiar Acts
are
beautiful
through
Love

– Percy Bysshe Shelley –

GRATITUDE AND PRIVILEGE

When we realise how privileged we are and that many others on this planet may not have the material wealth that we possess, we may feel confronted, or find our abundance difficult to understand. However, we needn't feel guilty, ashamed or undeserving.

Simply being thankful for all we have to enjoy in this life and contributing to our communities in active, meaningful ways makes a world of difference. By living mindfully and lovingly for ourselves and others, we extend loving energy outward into the world at large and actively contribute to the peace and happiness of our planet. In any case, the best things in life are free. Not all privilege is tangible; it is a state of the heart. The more we realise this, we begin to look at life, opportunity, peace and privilege in a whole new way. There is so much room for positive change in this world. Let it begin with you.

LOVE RESTS
ON NO FOUNDATION.

IT IS AN ENDLESS
OCEAN,

WITH NO BEGINNING
OR END.

- Rumi -

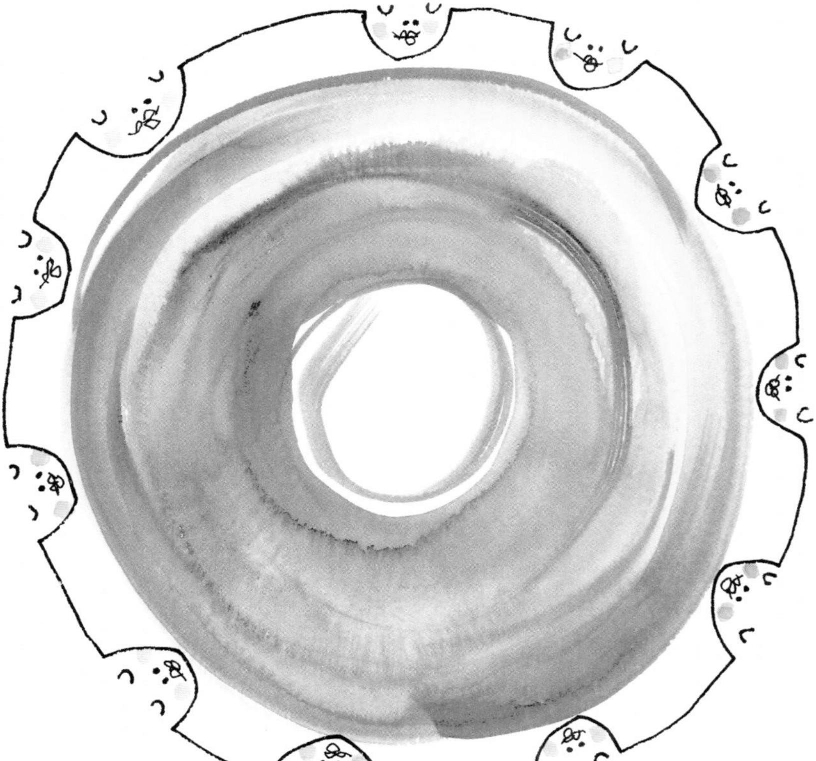

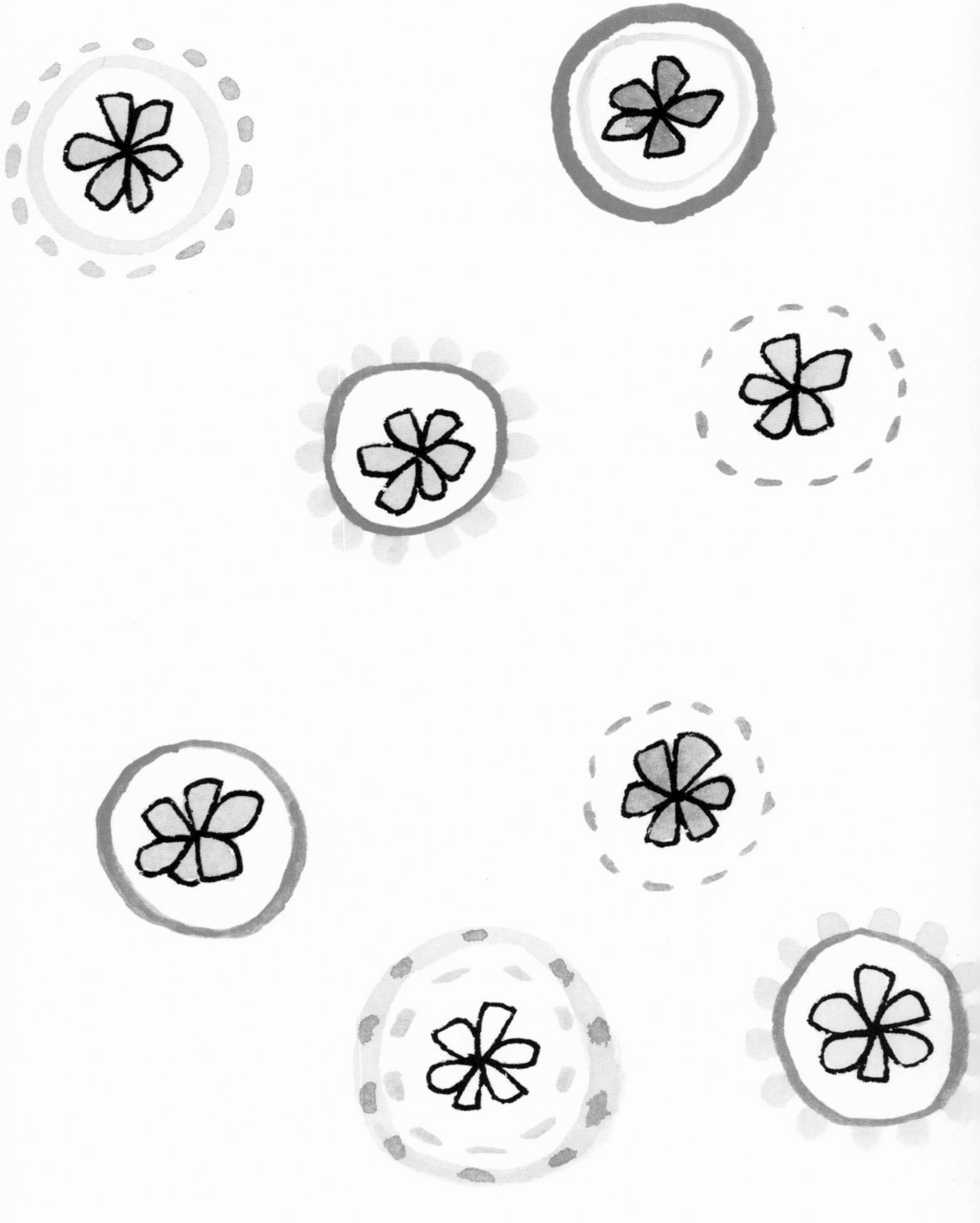

GRATITUDE and PRIORITIES

PRIORITISING GRATITUDE

Having a solid focus in life is a wonderfully grounding and motivating thing. Some people focus on fame or fortune, others on their relationships, jobs, families, possessions or aesthetics. Prioritising gratitude allows us to put all of these things into perspective and cultivate joy and harmony on every level.

When we love ourselves, we know what parts of our lives are not working for us and we let these parts drop away. We may actively need to make changes, and the ways to do so will become easily apparent as we are in tune with ourselves, others and the world around us. There is no situation beyond us. We are safe in ourselves when we love ourselves.

Prioritising gratitude means:

- Actively focusing on the positives
- Counting our blessings
- Coming from a place of love and appreciation
- Always respecting ourselves, others and life itself.

The big question is, when it comes to living, do you take things for granted or take them with gratitude?

Focusing on gratitude, being thankful in daily life for all we have and all we are, is the baseline for a happy life. See gratitude as your foundation and craft your reality from this point. Living like this, you will lead an amazing, fulfilling and love-filled life.

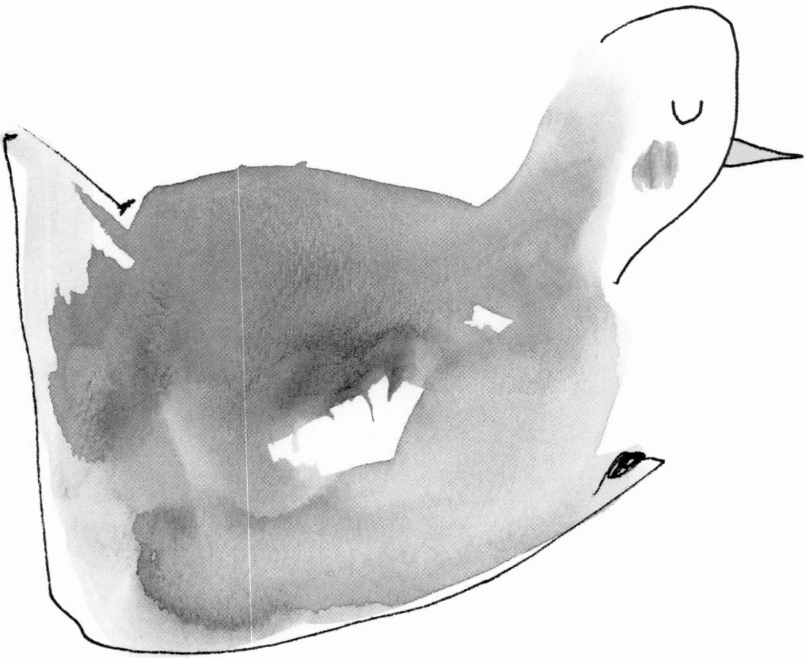

Today is the
first day
of the rest
of your life.

— Anon —

BALANCE

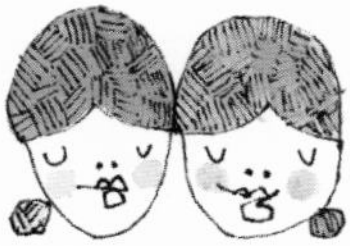

A balanced life feels good. It allows us time to work, play, indulge, rest and relax, and a chance to enjoy our hobbies and passions to the fullest. In experiencing all the elements of our lives, a balanced approach makes us happier and more satisfied human beings.

It is not about finding the time for balance, it is about making the time. This is an active and conscious decision crucial to our health and wellbeing.

- Balancing activity: Try this activity now. Make a list of the things you do on a typical day. Now mark a C next to each activity you consider a chore, and a P next to those you consider a pleasure.

- Too many Ps? Keep it up! Too many Cs? Maybe too much work and no play is making you intense and unhappy? Or maybe your thoughts need to shift to allow for more positive experiences? How can you let more joy in? Waking up fifteen minutes earlier and doing some gentle yoga might make a world of difference, as might planning a holiday, or taking those foreign language classes you've been putting off. Allow yourself the time to learn something new, put your feet up, or have a good giggle.

LIFE BALANCING ACTIVITY

C	P

When our lives are on track, our days are full of Ps. In loving life, even what we call 'work' becomes a 'P' for pleasure! Our thoughts can make all things a joy. There is always room for us to set fresh goals as we commit fully to living our best lives. Make these lists regularly as your life changes, and ensure that there are plenty of Ps to fill you with gratitude, balance your moods, nurture your health, and support your wellbeing.

'TO ENJOY' LIST

Rather than writing a typical **'TO DO'** list, try making and calling yours a **'TO ENJOY'** list. You will be amazed how shifting this emphasis will make a life changing difference.

GIVE ALL TO LOVE;

OBEY THY HEART.

Ralph Waldo Emerson

Whoso walketh in solitude,
And inhabiteth the wood,
Choosing light, wave, rock and bird,
Before the money-loving herd,
Into that forester shall pass
From these companions
power and grace.

– Ralph Waldo Emerson 'Woodnotes' –
Poems, 1847

FOLLOW YOUR HEART

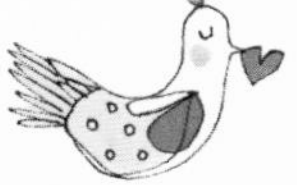

While we hear these three words all the time, how often are we brave enough to really hear them? Braver still, put them into action? Following our hearts is about really listening to our inner wisdom with gratitude. The marvellous truth is we always know the answer deep inside to any question we could ever have. We spend so much time asking for advice, looking at others, comparing, procrastinating and worrying. While positive sounding boards and good advice can be very helpful, when it comes to following our hearts, it comes to looking within.

Another way to say 'follow your heart' might be 'follow your bliss'. If it comes to your work, for example, think of a job you would almost do without being paid. Time flies when you do it. You dream about it, consider it your passion. You are thankful for it in your life. It feels natural. With relationships, listen to how your mind and body feel. Do you feel respected, safe, treasured and understood? Do things flow and make sense with your significant other, family member or friends? Do you feel an inner 'yes' that comforts and inspires you? Is your heart happy?

In every moment, relationship and experience, every day, we have the choice to follow our hearts. This choice is expressed through the words we speak, the actions we take and the thoughts we choose to think. Check in like this: if it feels light, easy and right, it's going with your heart. It if feels dark, heavy and uneasy, it's likely going against your heart's path. See overleaf for a Heart Centre Meditation guide.

When we follow our bliss, the dots of life connect. A path is built and a lantern lights our way. We are constantly supported by life when we follow our hearts, so go on, be brave! Be authentic, be satisfied and be happy.

HEART CENTRE MEDITATION

Another lovely, easy way to check in with your heart is to take a few deep breaths and put your hand on it. Do it now. Just feel your heart beating for a few moments. How easy is that, and how rarely do we do it?

Take a few more deep breaths and just feel your heart beat. Feel that you are alive. You might like to close your eyes.

Now ask your heart what it might like, or what would make it happy. You might ask 'What can I do for you?' You might not receive an answer immediately but you will get an answer! Look out for signs, symbols or flashes of clarity in following moments, hours or days. They will make sense to you. You will recognise them. You know what you want and need and life supports you. Thank your heart for nourishing and guiding you.

Do what
you love, and
love
what you do

GRATITUDE and STRESS RELIEF

STRESS

Stress is something we all experience, whether in our work, relationships, homes, travel, or other aspects of our worlds. Life just gets busy. Things pile up. We never switch off our phones. Unexpected events happen at critical moments. We mostly do a minimum of two things at once. We forget to take breaks.

Stress can feel like it's 'taking hold' of us, or 'carrying us away' to an unpleasant place both mentally and physically. We think, 'Once that's sorted I'll be able to relax' – then something new pops up. And our stress about stressing only compounds our despair!

Yet we are always in control.

How nice to see stress as an emotion that, like a crystal-clear stream, moves through our bodies as all emotions naturally do when we allow them the freedom to. We don't need to judge our emotions, just kindly let them move on through. Our calmer, inner wisdom always lights a new and more effective way forward when we take a second to be gentle with ourselves. Just a couple of moments' pause or a few deep breaths can make a real difference to our mental state and help us process thoughts and decisions with clarity.

We live in 3D and full colour. Emotions and experiences of all kinds make us rich, deep and connected human beings. If it's channelled wisely as it moves through us, stress can even help us identify our boundaries, our preferences and priorities. All experiences can work for us.

We actively choose our thoughts and can actively change them. Our thoughts create our realities so they're worth our daily TLC. Next time you feel stressed, affirm to yourself 'stress moves through me'. It won't stay circulating unless you allow it to. How powerful! Let's embrace the possibilities of relaxation in each moment and enjoy our lives to the fullest. In the words of Jacobus Johannes Leeuw 'The mystery of life is not a problem to be solved but a reality to be experienced.'

These roses under my window make no reference to former roses or to better ones; they simply are what they are... There is no time for them. There is simply the rose; it is perfect in every moment of its existence.

- Ralph Waldo Emerson -

ASKING FOR HELP

Asking for and accepting help when we need it is a natural part of day-to-day life. However, for many people it is a very hard thing to do. Some of us feel ashamed to say that we cannot manage everything alone, or we feel guilty for relying on others. Some of us want to control all situations and in our inflexibility, fear others' involvement. Life needn't be so difficult!

Asking for help is about recognising the value and love of others in our lives, appreciating our own time and energy, and honouring our need for rest. It is about being open to sharing, and inviting more love and support into our lives. Very simply, asking for and accepting help when needed contributes greatly to our health and happiness.

If we feel that we are constantly running after our spouses, our children, our friends or any others in our lives, we will soon feel drained. The simplest way for us to avoid feeling this way and guarantee we live happy, supported lives together is to get used to asking each other for help when we need it – and asking without guilt, shame or fear.

There are many positive ways to ask each other for help, ways in which we can even compliment each other by drawing on each other's skills and abilities. If we need our children to do more around our homes to make our lives easier, we can draw up colourful, fun itineraries as families detailing and designating daily jobs. Giving our children responsibilities honours their abilities, recognises their important role in family life, and strengthens both organisational and practical skills.

If we need our beloveds to lift their game and give us more support, we can find loving and positive ways to express these needs simply and clearly. We are all different. While some of us easily intuit the needs of others, others may require prompting. Speak from the heart: 'I'm finding it hard to manage this and it would really be wonderful for me if you could . . . Can you please help me?' You'll often be amazed at how someone who loves you will respond to this gentle request without you having to push any further. If nothing budges, it might be time for you to love yourself a little more and redefine your boundaries. Try exactly the same, simple approach with friends. Speak up, be clear about your needs, and learn to ask for and accept help. It is natural for us to share this life, to give and receive with ease, grace and gratitude.

YOU WERE
BORN
WITH WINGS.
WHY PREFER
TO CRAWL
THROUGH LIFE ?

- Rumi -

A HAPPY MAN IS TOO SATISFIED WITH THE PRESENT TO DWELL TOO MUCH ON THE FUTURE.

– Einstein –

VISUALISATIONS

These are my two favourite visualisations (or mini-meditations) for instant stress relief. I am always amazed at how grounding and effective these techniques are, and they are simple and clear enough to remember and use every day.

See overleaf for exercises

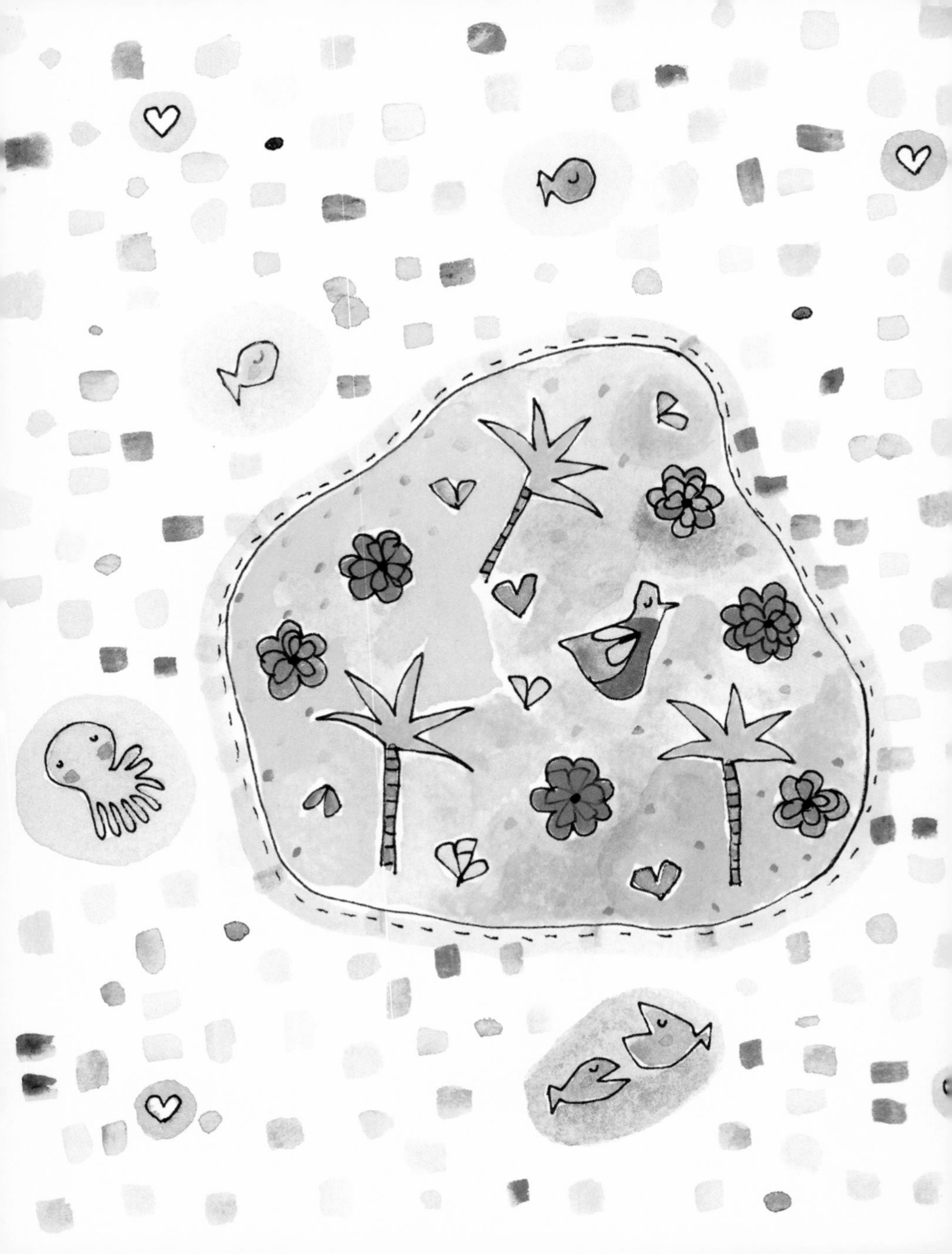

INNER ISLAND

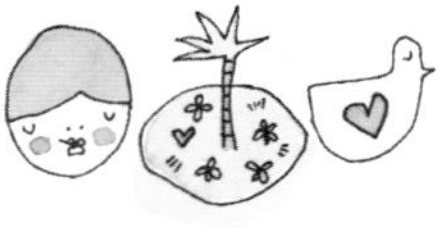

The first visualisation is an island within ourselves, or an 'inner island', a concept written about so beautifully by Thich Nhat Hahn in his book Happiness. *Our inner islands are our personal sanctuaries and are always there, waiting for us to visit.*

Get creative thinking about your inner island and visit it as often as you can. Your island might have abundant flowers, white sandy beaches, endless sunshine, palm trees, summer breezes, beautiful birds or thousands of stars in a clear sky above. Your island is yours and nobody can spoil it. I spend a lot of time on my island and can highly recommend it. You can go there when feeling overwhelmed, tired, or simply when needing some quality R&R. How good is this?

Close your eyes and go there now.

What does your island look like? What does it feel like? Visualise the details, the colours, scents and weather, the colour of the water and the feel of the sand. You might focus on the lusciousness of the palm trees, the sweetness of the coconuts . . .

Spend as much time as you can (or would like to) on your island, and when you open your eyes, take a few deep breaths to let the deeply relaxing benefits of your instant holiday sink in.

TREE ROOTS

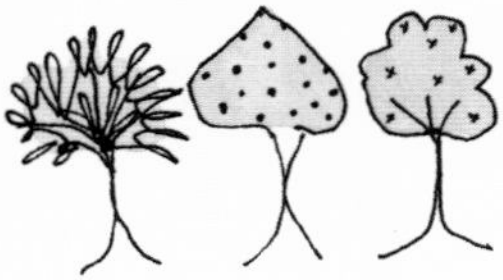

Have you ever watched a tree in a storm as its branches swing wildly about in the air while its roots are safe and protected in the soil?

Another of Thich Nhat Hahn's passages encourages us to see ourselves as possessing roots, or consciously existing at our root level. No matter what environmental forces may be causing havoc or distress in our outer world, we too have roots. We are grounded in ourselves. This image of the swinging branches with steady roots intact brings me enormous stability and calm in any stressful moment. I always imagine any outer chaos in my life as the wind rustling my branches, yet my inner world remains safe, nestled and grounded, like tree roots. Try this visualisation next time you feel the need to nurture or settle yourself. I hope it brings you the strength, peace and relief it always brings to me.

"I am old and
have known a
great many troubles,
but most of them
never happened."

– Anon –

FROM ADVERSITY

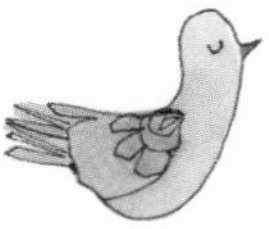

Have you ever noticed in nature where a tree or flower withers, a new little tree or bloom takes life in its place? So fast and fresh, so strong and healthy – a life affirming, joyous symbol of life and of constant renewal. It is equally moving to see how flowers can spring up from a concrete footpath, train track or brick wall. We needn't ever feel hopeless, life always prevails! It is nature's all encompassing way to fill gaps when and where they are created. Life triumphs with a miraculous rhythm, revealing to us its very own wisdom. When we relax with gratitude into the infinite richness of life's mystery and beauty, we can truly put aside our worries, trust deeply and live fully.

Just as in nature, regeneration and renewal are natural and necessary parts of our human experience. There are times we need to shed our leaves, times for budding, and times for blooming in all our magnificence. Our bodies' cells are in a constant state of renewal, as are our thoughts and feelings. If we are ever uprooted, destabilised or hurt, it is likely a moment for us to develop stronger roots in ourselves for our futures. If we take on life changes and challenges with gratitude and love for the lessons they bring, embrace rather than resist life, we may grow stronger than we may ever have imagined we could.

When we face adversities in our lives with gratitude for the deep and wise messages they bring, the positive changes they encourage us to make or the openings they create for us to grow, any life experience becomes a very rich journey. We may never understand the reason that we are presented with certain hardships, though if we trust in life, there is always something profound for us to gain. 'The best is yet to come', 'every cloud has a silver lining', 'there's light at the end of the tunnel' – these are very common ways of expressing the same life-affirming sentiment. Take comfort. Take strength.

STRESS AND SUPERFICIALITY

In this intensely visual world in which the way things look is often championed over other special qualities, it comes as no wonder that we all stress from time to time about appearances, namely our own.

Fixations on achieving a certain body shape or size, mastering a particular look, or pursuing 'ideal' beauty are the causes for much angst in many of our private worlds. It is not so common that we stop to thank our bodies, really thank ourselves with unconditional love, for just how well we are doing and how beautiful we truly are. We might never have done this before, and the thought of such self-praise can be uncomfortable. Just as infrequent are the moments we realise we are all actually miracles – walking, talking, breathing, feeling parts of nature. This extraordinary truth is so often taken for granted.

Have you ever felt stressed, sad or frustrated due to being judged on or valued by the way you look? Perhaps you have stopped to realise that you too are judging others almost instantly by the way they appear on the surface. Have you ever felt as if you need more possessions to feel good, then stopped to realise that they won't be the answer?

Like me, you might have wished for a deeper, more authentic kind of currency than the illusory, subjective market of 'beauty' or 'attractiveness'.

The truth is, most people want to look good. We all have the same worries. We want to be admired, we want to be liked, we want to feel good about ourselves. And we can – without the doubt and fear.

Gratitude for life and for ourselves (self-love) are the best beauty accessories. They make us glow inside and out. When we are grateful for life and love ourselves we commit to our health. We let go of the worry, do things that make us happy, and we glow. Our inner beauty radiates and is magnetic, inspiring and incredibly appealing to others.

By deciding that we don't want to stress any more about how we look, we free ourselves of worry, self-judgement and doubt. After all, how much worrying about how we look contributes toward our feeling good? Not one little bit. By freeing ourselves of this burden, we also free others to be who they are.

Nothing that we've ever felt in our pasts, no amount of awkwardness, exclusion, negative thinking or criticism, has to shape our futures unless we allow it to. From today on, the present, let go. Just let go. Commit fully to feeling really good about yourself. Every day. By radiating joy, gratitude, self-respect and wellbeing, you will look and feel as gorgeous and complete as you truly are.

True happiness is to enjoy the present, without anxious dependence upon the future, not to amuse ourselves with either hopes or fears but to rest satisfied with what we have, which is sufficient, for he that is so wants nothing. The greatest blessings of mankind are within us and within our reach. A wise man is content with his lot, whatever it may be, without wishing for what he has not.

- Attributed to Seneca -

GRATITUDE AND AFFIRMATIONS

AFFIRMATIONS

The practice of reading, writing, hearing or even singing affirmations is life-changing. As we are so often reminded, our thoughts create our worlds. Positive thoughts create a positive reality, negative thoughts create worlds full of negativity. We choose our thoughts, so we have the power!

Affirmations queen Louise Hay describes affirmations as statements of truth that, like seeds planted in the fertile soil of our minds, transform into our fully grown realities. Examples of affirmations might be: 'I am healthy, vibrant and strong', or 'I love and trust myself'.

While it may sound overly simplistic to use affirmations to change our lives and at first our conscious minds may even resist our words, if practised with commitment, affirmations work. By focusing on and reinforcing our positive, affirmative thoughts, they soon become completely natural and unquestioned realities in our minds. And as the old adage goes – mind over matter! Moreover, our subconscious minds have no sense of humour, so we must truly be mindful of our negative, self deprecating dialogue at all times, words and thoughts alike.

Start by taking pen to paper. Write five 'truths' you want to feel deeply and without reservation in your mind, body and life. These statements might not seem to be true at first, they might in fact sound ridiculous to us, but that is precisely why affirmations are required. We can become so accustomed to self-criticism and negative thinking, we don't even recognise positive, loving thoughts! 'I am beautiful.' 'I am loved.' 'I have all the support I need.' 'I trust myself completely.' 'I am great at everything I turn my hand to.' 'I am amazing just as I am.' And why shouldn't you be!? We were born to shine as human beings, not hide our lights under bushels!

Repeat your affirmations out loud in the mirror twice a day. Write them down morning and night, and if you feel inclined, draw or write them beautifully and stick them up in your favourite space so you are surrounded by them day to day. I draw mine and hang them on my walls, I write them on the shower screen and I listen to them in my earphones as I go walking. A new way I have found to create extraordinarily powerful affirmations, and an approach recommended by Louise Hay, is to record my own voice saying my 'truths' aloud and listening to them as regularly as possible. There is a strong sense of trust already established when our subconscious mind hears own our voice.

The mirror is a wonderful way to work with affirmations, as you'll see by the look in your eyes which truths need the most repetition! They are the hardest ones to say out loud and the ones that might make you feel a bit silly or self-conscious. These are the powerful ones. So wave goodbye to any old thoughts that affirmations might be embarrassing or useless. I used to recite mine quietly and alone in my studio, now I sing them out loud, no matter who might be listening! Be proud to know you are on your very own journey to be your best self. Let others support you in your positive thinking. Don't be bothered by others' reservations or criticisms – inside we all want amazing and completely fulfilled lives; some of us are just ready to go for it and make it happen.

The more you surround yourself with your very own personalised power thoughts, the more natural and normal they become. You will also find that you attract other people with a similar zest for life, and these people will love and support you as you flourish and they do too. You will naturally move away from those people in your life who deplete and repress you. Dream big, ask big, and trust that you are being divinely assisted each step of the way. There is much more magic in this world than meets the eye. Invite it to work especially for you.

PRACTISING AFFIRMATIONS

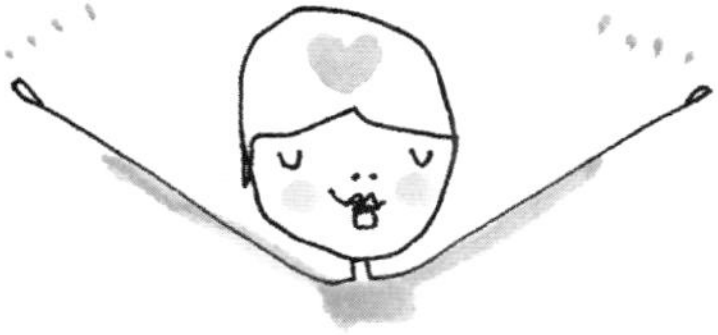

Life is a journey filled with joys and challenges of all kinds.

In order to live happily, we must constantly recommit our connection to and trust in life. This is an exercise in gratitude and deep love.

Practising affirmations is a simple and transformative practice in good times as well as trying times.

Practising positive affirmations in great moments helps us to accept all the good in our worlds and positively reinforces our right to feel amazing! I thank Louise Hay for her inspiration in guiding the following words.

AFFIRMATIONS

Here are some simple starter affirmations to transform, soothe, comfort and inspire.

♡

TIREDNESS	I have all the energy and support I need.
SADNESS	I am carried every day. I am never alone.
LONELINESS	I am loved and lovable.
PAIN	My body knows what to do. In every moment, I heal myself.
Lack of Inspiration	My life is beautiful. I notice the details. My ideas flow.
FEAR	I am safe. Life loves me.
DOUBT	I know exactly what to do.
Worry	My life runs smoothly. I relax.
PERFECTIONISM	I am good enough just as I am. I approve of myself.

POSITIVE REINFORCEMENT AFFIRMATIONS

These affirmations positively reinforce our right to feel amazing and to deserve all the good in our lives.

HAPPINESS	Happiness is my divine right.
ease	I flow through life with ease.
CONFIDENCE	I believe in myself. Life supports me.
COURAGE	I trust myself. I can do this.
Clarity	I think and see clearly.
SUCCESS	I deserve all the good in my life. I congratulate myself.
ENERGY	I am full of radiant energy. I love life. I nurture and honour my mind and body.
♥ COMFORT	I deserve all the comforts in my life and embrace them with gratitude. I am happy and at peace in myself.

THE PRESENT MOMENT IS WHERE YOUR PAST MEETS YOUR FUTURE. TRANSFORMATION IS YOURS TO EMBRACE IN THIS VERY MOMENT.

Inspired by

Thich Nhat Hanh

MY OWN AFFIRMATIONS

Use this free space to create your own affirmations. Be brave, bold, gentle, honest and free! This is your life. ♡

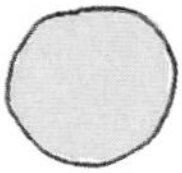

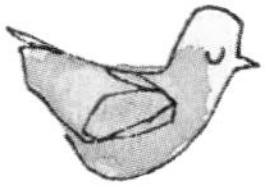

From this day on I will
live my life in gratitude.
I will love the rainbows for
colouring my world, the rain for
nourishing my inner garden.
I will highlight the joys for showing
me love, I will honour the hard
times for showing me strength.
I will welcome happiness and praise
as they are my dues, I will invite
new challenges to help me grow.
I will wake each morning in love with
myself and in love with life.

– Meredith –
Inspired by Og Mandino

GRATITUDE and SUSTAINABLE HAPPINESS

SUSTAINING OUR DAILY HAPPINESS – GRATITUDE AS A RENEWABLE RESOURCE

We are with ourselves for life, so we need to first love and appreciate ourselves. We can then love each other and the world around us, and enjoy happy, healthy and fulfilling lives.

Have you ever thought, 'I'm feeling happy now, this is amazing, but it won't last'? We are often so stuck in self-sabotaging thoughts, albeit unconsciously, that it can feel unrealistic to expect lasting good in our lives. We assume we cannot be happy forever. Yet life was not meant to be an impossible mission. The moment we realise that life is for us, not against us, we are open. We are able to flow. Gratitude helps us to see the good in every moment and to trust fully in life.

Gratitude is also a renewable resource. We will never run out of reasons to be grateful in life, nor lose our ability to tap into gratitude to shape and enhance our experience in any moment. We make our own luck, and we create our own happiness. When people say 'lucky' I always hear 'blessed'. I always know that either I or the other person have been creating their abundance from a place of self-love and self-respect. We have a right to expect lasting happiness and health, and when we truly love ourselves, we lead positively energised lives.

Like all relationships, our relationships with ourselves are like flowers that need love and care to blossom. By practising positive affirmations daily, by honouring our need for time, space, rest and relaxation, by being deeply grateful for all we have and are, we nurture ourselves. This is a way of life, a daily commitment. In each loving way we treat ourselves, each tender, caring moment we give to ourselves, we grow stronger. By knowing ourselves, trusting ourselves, appreciating ourselves and reaffirming the goodness of our lives, we experience sustainable happiness. This is a kind of happiness that no-one can ever take away from us as it is deeply and truly ours. Nurturing this happiness daily is such a joy and feels so good that it becomes a lifestyle choice we will never want to change!

There is an old saying, 'There are only two ways to live your life. One is as though nothing is a miracle. The other is as though everything is a miracle.' When people ask me 'Are you always happy?' I think 'yes'. But this isn't to say I do not, like all human beings, experience hardships or challenges. When I look at my personal experiences, I see all the parts of my life that have seemed most trying as the most character-building and enriching. They were all moments to cultivate the power of gratitude.

When I had a period of chronic illness I learnt about rest and relaxation. I learnt to love and be deeply grateful for my body. I learnt new ways to look after myself including adjusting my diet and practising regular yoga and meditation. When people I have loved have passed over I have continued to talk with them, feeling them around me and connecting with the mystery and beauty of life. When I have felt under stress moving house or country I have realised I take myself with me, and within myself I am home. When I have grieved for injustices beyond my world and reality, I have reinforced my resolve to live in gratitude for all I have, and to share as much love as is possible in this life. Gratitude is a sustainable and joyous way of life like no other.

THE BEST AND
MOST BEAUTIFUL
THINGS IN THE
WORLD CAN NOT BE
SEEN OR EVEN TOUCHED,
BUT JUST
FELT
IN THE HEART.

– Helen Keller –

TO LIVE IS
THE RAREST
THING IN
THE WORLD.
MOST PEOPLE
EXIST,
THAT IS ALL.

– Inspired by
Oscar Wilde –

ON GRATITUDE AND CHOOSING HAPPINESS

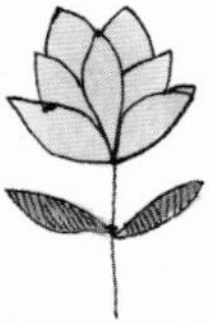

By choosing happiness we needn't suppress our other emotions. A dynamic and full spectrum of thoughts and feelings naturally constitute our daily lives. Pushing ourselves out of a natural cycle of emotions can lead to self-deprecation and feelings of failure or worry. It is not realistic for anybody to be happy all the time. Life is full, rich, balanced and complete in light and darkness, day and night, all the four seasons, laughter, tears, stillness and growth.

Feelings and thoughts are simply natural energy in motion. Seeing and experiencing this, we begin to sense challenging or uncomfortable feelings entering and exiting in constant flow, rather than lingering and creating blockages to inhibit or deplete us. We could say that all our passing emotions and feelings have a place, and yet no place at all – they move through us. Our thoughts and feelings needn't be categorised as good or bad, positive or negative, they simply are. It is stressful internal and external dialogues mixed with various expectations that cause our distress, and it takes practice to stop judging ourselves as harshly as all too often becomes habit. We judge ourselves in ways we would likely not judge others, and this contributes enormously to our collective unease. To feel upset and then feel bad about feeling upset only compounds our problem! When we honour ourselves for feeling how we feel, identify the reason as best as we can and reinforce our commitment to loving ourselves and life, we may move through and grow from any challenge facing us with strength and grace.

Recognising and catching counterproductive, judgemental or self-sabotaging thoughts and feelings allows us to intercept and transform them. This process is an opportunity for personal growth and an exercise in living mindfully. Through all the grateful approaches and choices expanded upon within this book, ones we can live and breathe simply and without fuss, we may come to a place where we can see our own power to choose in life from a place of self-love. This is a remarkable power we may never have known we possessed, and happiness naturally follows.

Staying strong on our ability to choose happiness is deeply empowering, and is very much supported by the principles of mindfulness and mindfulness meditation. For further information on this bountiful and inspiring theme, please see the 'Mind and Mindfulness' Recommended Resources list at the back of this book.

Stress, for example, is often perceived as a 'negative' feeling or experience, but it can also be a motivating force, or an impetus for creating healthier boundaries for ourselves in daily life (see page 134). By living in gratitude we are able to put the joys and pleasures of our lives into focus, allow them to become magnified, and find a sustainable reservoir of positive energy, peace and joy from which to draw daily strength and inspiration.

Gratitude is no sugar coating, it is a way of life. Unconditional self-love is the foundation for a fulfilling, contented path and is all founded in gratitude for ourselves and our lives. Practising self-love until it becomes an unthinking, natural habit means moving away from relentless, often unrecognised self-criticism, noticing the crippling effects of perfectionism and being deeply kind to ourselves. (See Chapter One on Self-Love and Gratitude, page 31.) With self-love, we may indeed find lasting happiness, and continue to choose and create it consciously for ourselves. It is possible for all of us to make positive changes from a place of self-love rather than self-criticism. Judging our feelings and ourselves in negative ways naturally comes to a halt when we deeply love and accept ourselves.

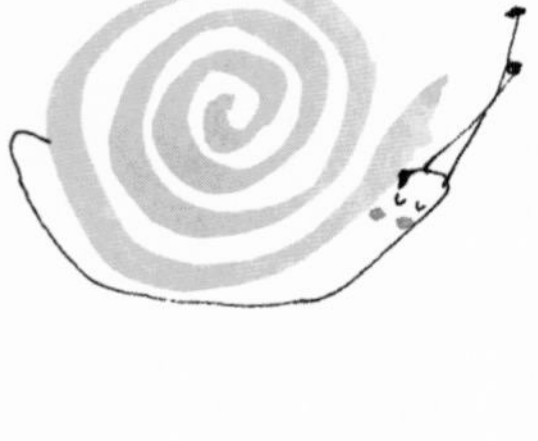

A Word on Wellbeing

Some people may find it hard to relax and enjoy life, no matter how hard they try. Such suffering warrants special care and attention. It is always encouraged that people in profound distress seek help, as they may benefit enormously from a combination of medical intervention and mindfulness/relaxation therapies. A **great many others** are simply world weary, self deprecating, overwhelmed, overworked and disconnected from themselves, others and nature. For these people, a conscious shift in focus is nothing short of life changing. **My hope is that** we will find choosing gratitude an immediately available, supportive, encouraging and endless resource for the rest of our lives.

Try not to change
the world.
You will fail.
Try to love the world.
Lo, the world is changed.

- Sri Chinmoy -

LOVING EARTH – GRATITUDE AS THE FOUNDATION FOR WORLD PEACE

Just as happiness comes from within, peace starts with us too. Gratitude is the open door to abundance and vitality. When we love ourselves and see ourselves as part of nature, we naturally want to love and support our planet. We want to do the least harm. We want to nurture and protect rather than burn, destroy, pillage and spoil. When we are truly grateful for our earth, these things become unthinkable. We are at one with the world around us, and it is our responsibility and our privilege to care for our earth.

From little things big things grow. While the byproduct of living thankfully is an all encompassing improvement in life as we know it, actively practicing gratitude is a process that starts with small, simple and achievable changes in our thinking. If each human being were to trust her or himself and live in gratitude and love, our life experiences on a global level would be transformed beyond recognition. We can never underestimate the power we possess. This philosophy is reinforced beautifully by the famous words attributed to Mahatma Gandhi, 'Be the change you want to see in the world.' By simply recognising and respecting the precious beauty of life and nature, we begin.

There are certain things in this world over which we have very little control, but we can always start within. With our thoughts. We can live by example and generate light for others to feel safe, secure and joyous in their own lives. With our commitment to life, we live in gratitude. With our inner peace we give others comfort. With our enthusiasm for life, we inspire ourselves and others. Through our learning, we grow and share our understanding. With our appreciation of all that we are and all that we have, we are rich beyond words. My dream and constant affirmation is to see this world as a happy, healthy and loving place where all beings are respected and living in harmony.

We are truly empowered, just by being alive. We can all be instruments of peace, simply by choosing to love and be grateful for ourselves, each other and our world. It's this simple. And it starts here.

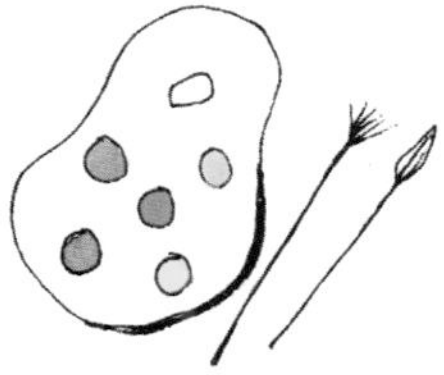

MY COUNTRY
IS THE WORLD,
AND MY RELIGION
IS TO DO GOOD.

— Thomas Paine —

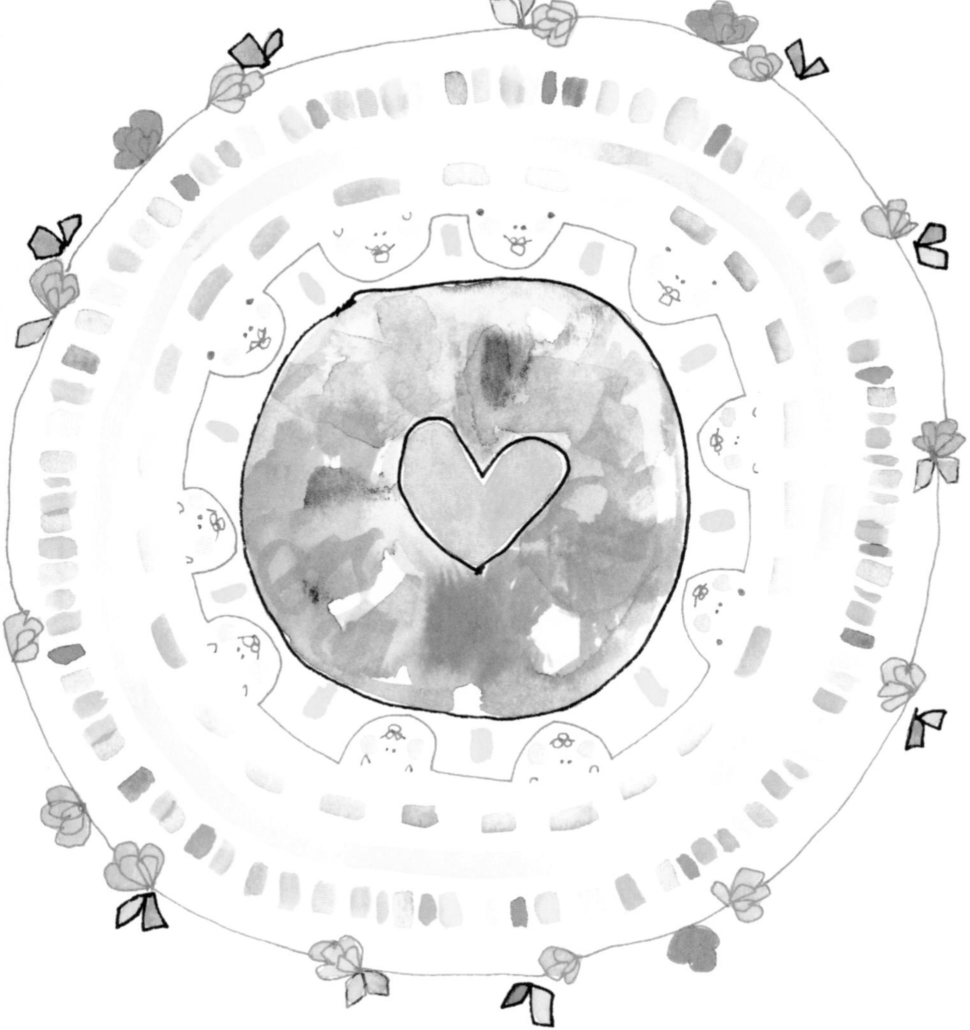

Closing note

Living gratefully is a deeply joyous, rewarding and transformative way of life. I hope you have enjoyed this little book, filled to the brim with inspirations and ideas, and that you have made it your own by writing, drawing, listing and growing your own thoughts and dreams within. May this celebration of gratitude inspire you to live an amazing life, taking responsibility for designing a truly wonderful, fulfilling reality for yourself. Those you love will want to know your secret as you glow on into the brightest future imaginable!

Congratulate yourself on taking the time to count your blessings each day and invite even more beauty and joy into your life. You are contributing to a happier, healthier and more peaceful world for all by living so mindfully and with such love.

To read on or access some exciting tools to support you on your path, please find a list of recommended resources on page 188. I hope these suggestions bring you as much support and inspiration as they have brought me.

Embrace all things with love and love will embrace you.

Meredith

RECOMMENDED RESOURCES

I am very thankful for each of these resources and their respective writers and creators. Each book, audio program or website listed below has left a real imprint on me, teaching me something new and changing my life.

While I could not list all the books relating to gratitude that I have ever loved, I hope this list will provide inspiration for your further reading. My world has been so enhanced by reading and learning new things across a variety of genres and subject matter, and my journey to live a happy and healthy life inspires my endless curiosity. I hope you may enjoy sharing in some of these wonderful books and tools.

Books

Mind and Mindfulness

Answers from the Heart – Thich Nhat Hanh

Be Free Where You Are – Thich Nhat Hanh

The Biology of Belief – Bruce Lipton

The Brain that Changes Itself – Norman Doidge

The Divided Mind – Donald Epstein

Full Catastrophe Living – Jon Kabat-Zinn

Happiness: Essential mindfulness practices – Thich Nhat Hanh

Happiness and How It Happens – The Happy Buddha

The Honeymoon Effect: The science of creating heaven on earth – Bruce Lipton

How to Relax – Thich Nhat Hanh

Meditations: Food for the soul – Sri Chimnoy, 1970

Mindfulness and the Natural World: Bringing our attention back to nature – Claire Thompson

No Mud No Lotus – Thich Nhat Hanh

Nourishing Wisdom – Marc David

The Organised Mind: Thinking straight in the age of information overload – Daniel Levitan

Peace of Mind – Thich Nhat Hanh

The Secret of Secrets: On the secret of the golden flower – Osho

Seeds for a Boundless Life: Zen teaching from the heart – Zenkei Blanche Hartman
Seeking Silence in a Noisy World – Adam Ford
Starbright Series: Meditations for children – Maureen Garth
Thanks: How the new science of gratitude can make you happier – Robert Emmons
Thinking, Fast and Slow – Daniel Kahneman Thompson
You Can Heal Your Life – Louise Hay
You Were Not Born to Suffer – Blake D Bauer
Zen in the Garden – Zachia Zariah

Inspiration

101 Moments of Joy and Inspiration – Meredith Gaston
101 Inspirations for Your Journey – Meredith Gaston
The Art of Happiness – The Dalai Lama
Beyond Religion – The Dalai Lama
The BFG – Roald Dahl
The Complete Collected Poems – Maya Angelou
The Curly Pyjama Letters – Michael Leunig
Daphnis and Chloe – Illustrated by Marc Chagall
A Deep Breath of Life: Daily Reflections – Alan Cohen
Essays and Poems – Ralph Waldo Emerson, Barnes & Noble Classics series
The Essential Rumi – Coleman Barks

Grandiflora Celebrations – Saskia Havekes
The Happiest Refugee – Anh Do
How to Decorate – Shannon Fricke
I Am Here Now – The Mindfulness Project
I Know Why the Caged Bird Sings – Maya Angelou
Italian Joy – Carla Coulson
Letters to my Daughter – Maya Angelou
The Little Prince – Antoine de Saint Exupery
Love Gratitude – Joel Goldsmith
The Man With Dancing Eyes – Sophie Dahl
My Greek Island Life – Claire Lloyd
Shelter: How Australians Live – Kara Rosenlund
Start Something That Matters – Blake Mycoskie
Story of My Life – Helen Keller
Tucked In – Meredith Gaston
Wabi-Sabi for Artists and Designers – Leonard Koren

Journaling and self-expression

A Long Rainy Season: Women's Haiku – Liza Lowitz and Miyuki Aoyama
An Illustrated Life – Danny Gregory
Basho: Haiku compilation – Jane Reichhold
Diaries of Paul Klee – Paul Klee, edited by Felix Klee

Expression through art – Misty Mawn

The Gratitude Diaries – Janice Kaplan

How to be an Explorer of the World: Portable life museum – Keri Smith

Rumi: The Book of Love – Translation and commentary by Coleman Barks

Love and Clutter – Mirka Mora

Brave on Rocks; The True and the Questions; Spilling Open & Messy, Thrilling Life; And the Story is Happening – Illustrated journal series by Sabrina Ward Harrison

The Creative License – Danny Gregory

The Mindfulness Colouring In book – Emma Farrarons

This I Know: Notes on unraveling the heart – Susannah Conway

Unfurling, a Mixed Media Workshop with Misty Mawn: Inspiration and techniques for self-expression through art – Misty Mawn

Wicked but Virtuous – Mirka Mora

Wild Surrender: A journey into painting, poetry and life – Mindy Lacefield

Wreck This Journal – Keri Smith

Health and Wellbeing

12 Stages of Healing – Donald Epstein

The Art of Tidying Up: How to declutter your life – Kim Carruthers

Aussie Body Detox Diet – Saimaa Miller

The Body Keeps the Score: The transformation of trauma – Bessel Van der Kolk

Deliciously Ella – Ella Woodward

Eat Clean, Green and Vegetarian – Lee Holmes
Eat Yourself Beautiful – Lee Holmes
Elixir – Janella Purcell
Emotional Intelligence – Daniel Coleman
Energy Medicine – Donna Eden and David Feinstein
Fear: Essential wisdom for getting through the storm – Thich Nhat Hanh
The Green Kitchen Cookbook – David Frenkeil and Louise Vindahl
Healing Myths, Healing Magic – Donald Epstein
Healing With Wholefoods: Asian traditions and modern medicine – Paul Pitchford
The Medicinal Chef – Dale Pinnock
Mindful Eating, Mindful Life – Thich Nhat Hanh
My Family Table – Eleanor Ozich
My New Roots – Sarah Britton
Near and Far – Heidi Swanson
Organic – Don Burke
Petite Kitchen Cookbook – Eleanor Ozich
A Pukka Life – Sebastian Pole
Subtle Body – Cyndi Dale
Super Natural Every Day – Heidi Swanson
Supercharged Food – Lee Holmes
Women's Bodies, Women's Wisdom – Christiane Northrup, M.D.
The Yoga Tree – B.K.S Iyengar

Web

meredithgaston.com

The Daily Guru

My New Roots

Deliciously Ella

Green Kitchen Stories

Hay House

Supercharged Food

Mind Body Green

Audio

Jon Kabat-Zinn Mindfulness Meditation Tapes

Louise Hay talk: *How to Love Yourself*

Louise Hay Affirmations:

101 Power Thoughts for Life

Morning and Evening Affirmations

Self-confidence and Self-esteem

Feeling Fine

Enjoy your
life to the
full!

THANK YOU!

This book would not be quite the same without the loving support of these people: Julie Gibbs, Arielle Gamble, Katrina O'Brien, Jocelyn Hungerford and the whole team at Penguin Random House. Thank you all very much. To Arielle, whose magical hands and eyes have helped shape these pages, I treasure you.

Thank you to Mick Smith and his team at Splitting Image for ensuring these colours and lines sing in print.

To my husband Kevin and my family and friends for their encouragement and care, and to all the wise and brilliant thinkers, poets, artists and dreamers whose words and ideas feature amongst these pages. I continue to learn so much the more curious and passionate I become!

This book is dedicated to my beautiful mother Roslyn, who gave me life and so many reasons to be grateful. ♡

THIS DANCE

IS THE JOY

OF EXISTENCE

Rumi

LANTERN

UK | USA | Canada | Ireland | Australia
India | New Zealand | South Africa | China
Penguin Books is part of the Penguin Random House group of companies whose addresses can be found at global.penguinrandomhouse.com

First published by Penguin Australia Pty Ltd, 2016

Cover design by Arielle Gamble and Meredith Gaston
and text design by Arielle Gamble
© Penguin Australia pty. Ltd.
Illustrations by Meredith Gaston
Typeset in Caslon 9.5pt by 15
Colour separation by Splitting Image Colour Studio, Clayton, Victoria
Printed in China by RR Donnelley Asia Printing Solutions Limited.

National Library of Australia
Cataloguing-in-Publication data:

Creator : Gaston, Meredith, author.
Title : The Art of Gratitude / Meredith Gaston
ISBN: 9781921384103 (hardback)
Subjects : Gratitude -- Quotations, maxims, etc.
Gratitude in art. Life skills.
Dewey Number: 179.9

penguin.com.au/lantern

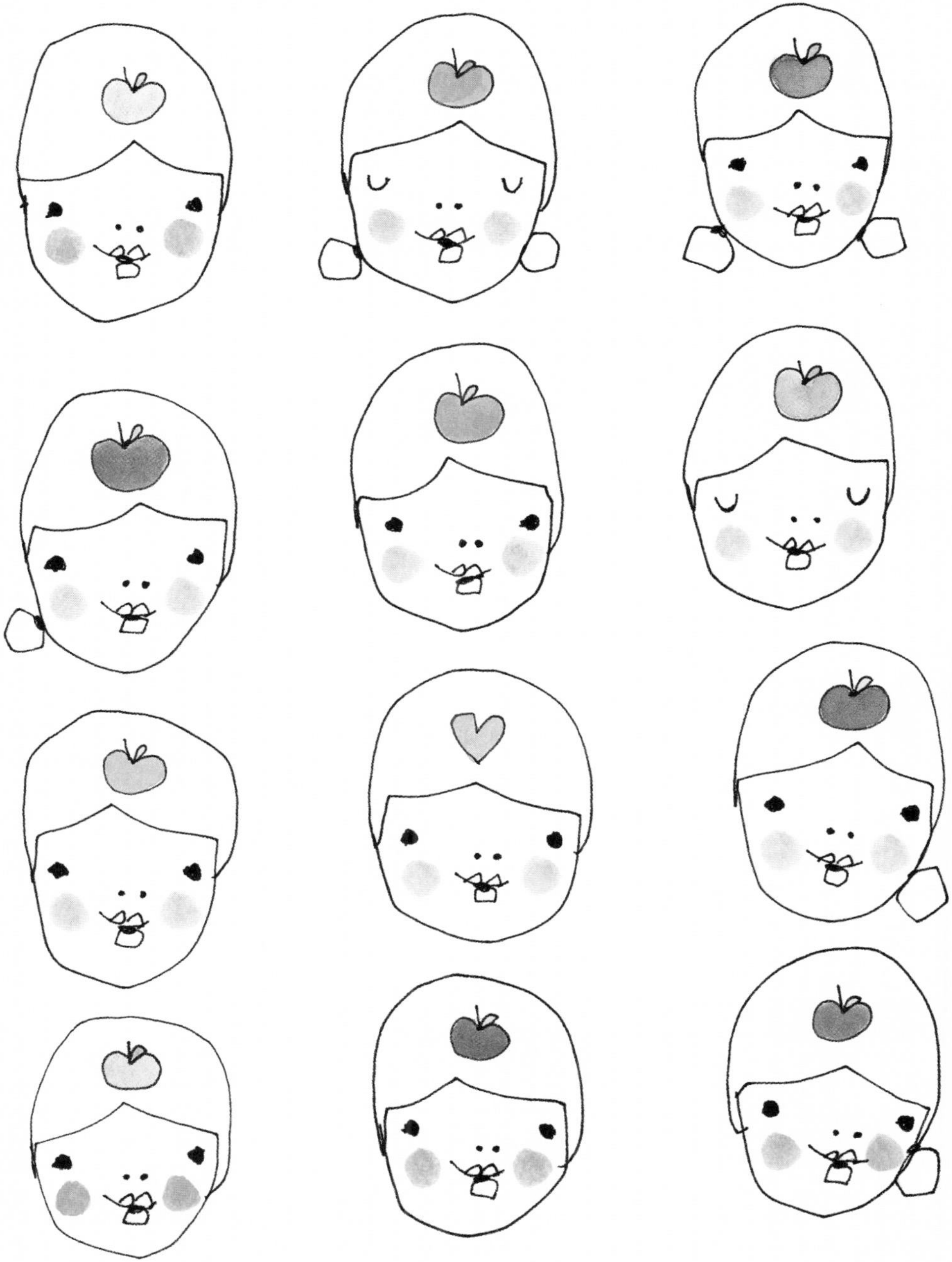

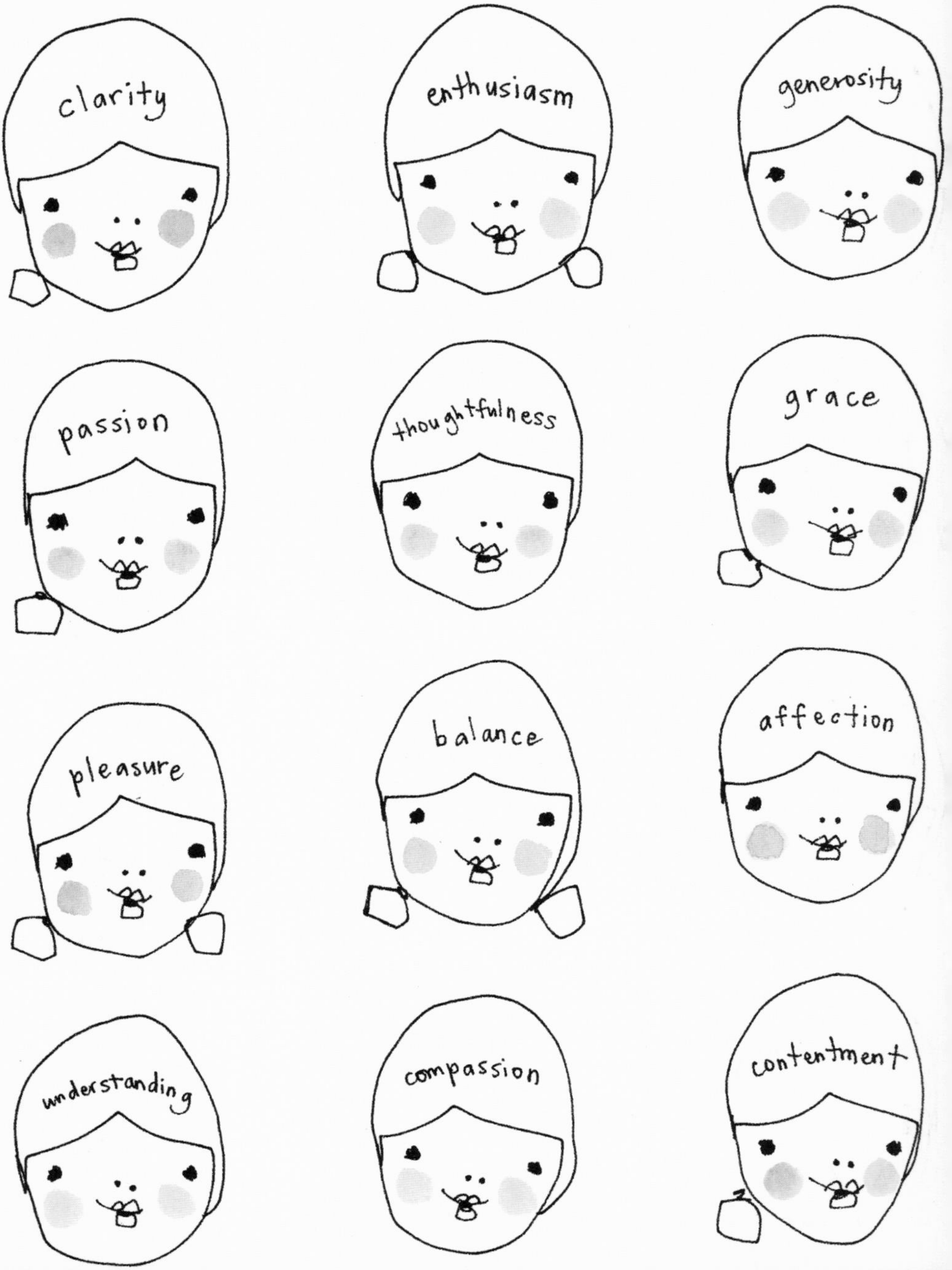
clarity
enthusiasm
generosity
passion
thoughtfulness
grace
pleasure
balance
affection
understanding
compassion
contentment